The 24
GREATEST FLIES
YOU DON'T LEAVE HOME WITHOUT
(An Indispensable Guide!)

Robert J. Sousa, Ph.D.

HUSKING BEE BOOKS
WARREN, RHODE ISLAND

10 9 8 7 6 5 4 3 2 1

ISBN: 978-0-615-32120-2

Library of Congress Control Number: 2010927108

Sousa, Robert J.
    The 24 Greatest Flies You Don't Leave Home Without
    Includes index.

1. Fly Fishing. I. Title

Questions regarding the content or ordering of this book should be
addressed to:
Husking Bee Books
P.O. Box 515
Warren, RI 02885
www.huskingbeebooks.com

Unless otherwise noted, all photographs by the author.
Individual fly photos in Chapter 3 by Umpqua Feather Merchants, Inc.
and printed with permission.

Printed in China

Cover design & illustrations: Tom Culora
Editing & layout: Jill Culora

CONTENTS

PREFACE

Within the fishing tackle industry there is a saying that there are lures made for fishermen and there are lures made for fish. This adage certainly applies to fly fishing. While fly fishing has been around for many hundreds of years, it began a modern era when in 1425 Benedictine abbess Dame Juliana Berners first used a dozen fly patterns to put fresh fish on the Sopwell England abbey's table. Since then, thousands of patterns have been contrived to take advantage of every nuance of fish predator and prey behavior.

An angler today can buy or make flies in all sorts of shapes, colors and sizes. Each new issue of every fly fishing magazine continues to parade before us new patterns that beg to catch every fish in the river, lake or ocean. Angling catalogs dangle new concoctions to see if we will take. Enough already, my fly boxes are full and I can't possibly carry any more patterns.

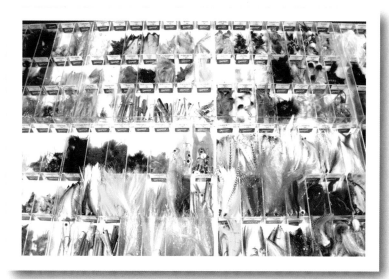

A grand display of large and colorful flies.

How can we possibly make some sense of all of this diversity? While most of the flies in the catalogs will catch fish, how can we filter the great flies from the many that are available? Don't fret; let's explore a reasonable solution.

A typical display of many small freshwater flies.

If you were to ask a thousand seasoned and successful fly anglers what flies they use, they would tell you that they catch most of their fish on a few favorite patterns. These anglers over many years have refined their selections to those flies proven to catch fish. Moreover, they have confidence in when, where and how to fish them. Remarkably, you would be surprised that the list for a seasoned angler is often quite short — generally about five or six flies.

Now, if it were true that most anglers catch most of their fish when they use about six flies and if we could compile a list of the six favorite flies of many accomplished anglers, we would have a fantastic fly box. The great revelation of this master list is that it would be far shorter than we might first expect. The reason is that many different anglers would list many of the same fly patterns. In other words, there is often quite a big overlap between preferred flies from one angler to another. I am proposing a total of 24 fantastic time-tested fly patterns.

I am applying my numerous years of fishing experience with many excellent anglers to assemble for you a simplified list of fly patterns that will help you catch most fish most of the time. While a given angler might dispute my list, no one can challenge the general effectiveness of each fly listed. The pattern has proved itself time and time again. As you become more accomplished in fly fishing, I am sure you will want to add additional fly patterns to your arsenal. Nevertheless, the flies highlighted here will serve you very well during your initial years in the sport, and even well beyond that!

Herewith then are the two dozen "go-to" flies that will catch fish in most places anywhere in the world. This book identifies those flies and provides critical insight on why they are successful. We discuss fish habitat and selected fish behaviors to refine why, when and where your fly selection will have the greatest likelihood of success. Fly fishing tips are offered throughout the book including how to recognize specific fish feeding behaviors, select a fly or even when to change flies to take advantage of a unique situation. With this information, you will be well on your way to becoming an accomplished fly angler and your catch rate will improve dramatically.

As a beginning fly tier, please remember that even imperfectly tied flies may catch fish and, in fact, may have some advantages reflecting that nature itself can at times be fretfully imperfect. Fly tying guru Jay "Fishy" Fullum states that complicated patterns take longer to tie requiring more steps and materials yet do not always catch more fish. Keep it simple. Veteran fly anglers will often relate examples of a fly's increased ability to catch fish as it continues to unravel and fall apart. Predators really do seek out and select the young, naive, wounded or infirmed prey. They are easy targets and, as a result, an easy meal. An ugly poorly tied or mangled fly can sometimes suggest to a fish something that resembles fish food. Some patterns even try to take advantage of that implausible simplistic trait; for example, Gary LaFontaine's *The Mess*, Brad Jackson's *Ugly Bug*, and the fly that nobody seems to claim, the *Yuk Bug*.

INTRODUCTION

Investment gurus will tell you that owning more of the same kinds of assets is not diversification. A few well-chosen investments, spread across a broad array of asset categories will more closely provide responsible market diversification within your risk appetite. Just like investing, a successful fly angler will manage the risk of being skunked or going home without having caught anything. By bringing with them and knowing where and how to use several exceptional, albeit different, patterns, risk is reduced greatly. In this book we explore those blue chip patterns and give you some idea when to use each of them.

I try to interpret what a fish might believe your presentation to be and hopefully it decides it is something it wants to eat. Of course, as in the game of football, you alone can call the play. You must make the fly selection, tie it onto your tippet securely, present it in the right place and make it look natural or, at least, provoke a primordial eating response. Remember this isn't so difficult because most fish, most of the time, are looking for something to eat.

Fly fishing is an interactive sport. Somewhat akin to golf, no two situations are exactly alike; fly fishing requires the angler to be involved in actually catching a fish. Stealth, concentration, planning, fly selection and an accurate cast are much more effective skills than a noisy bumbling angler casting without purpose at distances exceeding 90 feet. Further, unlike bait fishing which often is a passive activity where the bait attracts a fish to the hook using smell, color or the movement of the bait itself, fly fishing requires the angler to participate in luring the fish to the hook. Each presentation of the fly is a dynamic interaction, poetry if you wish, between the angler, the fly and the fish. A competent fly angler, like a competent golfer, is always thinking about how to take advantage of each and every situation. Each cast is important. Getting into position undetected to make that great presentation is a skill all anglers have to develop. Time on the water is valuable and good anglers want to use each moment effectively.

A small river with pocket water behind in-stream boulders can be a beautiful thing during the early spring.

For the angler's part, there are skills that need to be learned and used to ensure that the best fly is delivered to where the fish are most likely to be. To begin, an angler must have a balanced fly rod, reel, line, tapered leader and fly suited to effectively catch fish of the desired size and species. The angler must be able to cast 30 feet of fly line somewhat accurately and be able to recognize where the fish they are seeking are sure to be.

Equally important is when the fish actually takes your fly. You must develop good line control techniques in order to set the hook effectively before the fish spits out your lure. We discuss these skills early on to ensure that you have the basic information you need well before you reach the water.

Of course, the major component is the fly. Fly selection, or which fly you choose to tie onto your line, can be critical for some species. Also, how you actually fish a fly can make the difference between a hook up or a pass by the fish. For example, sometimes a fly is made to lie still on the water or at other times an angler must make it twitch, swim or make it appear to be seeking shelter. Remember that for the most part, our flies do not have the attractive smells that are inherent in bait fishing. Neither do they typically spin, buzz or rattle as is common to some typical fishing lures. Consequently, successful fly fishing is a direct relationship between the presentation and the action of the fly, its shape, profile, size and color, and fish behavior. Each factor has to be considered, at least at a subliminal level, by the angler on every cast. While we might not be able to control what the fish might do, our ability to control the fly selection, where we place the fly and how it behaves after the presentation and line control is what makes this sport unique. If we do it right, we catch fish!

Stream, bay or lake side, you may want or need to cast to a precise spot upon the water. At other times an angler, by tracking a series of sequential surface rises, makes a delivery to a location where the fish is going to be in a moment or two. Lastly, because you may not be able to see beneath the water's surface, search casting to many likely spots may be the only strategy available. Knowing where to find fish and where you are most likely to catch one is a function of fish habitat and fish behavior. Fish live where they do for a reason. They know the kinds of water flows, structure or other habitat conditions most likely to deliver a meal. In order to effectively find fish, you need to ensure that you have some skill in determining the best habitats for the fish species you are seeking. That said, successfully delivering the fly to a fish — in a way that

xiv THE 24 GREATEST FLIES YOU DON'T LEAVE HOME WITHOUT

appears natural — completes the process.

Now while all this might seem complicated, don't be discouraged. There are a lot of things in the angler's favor. For example, a fish is not the brightest bulb in the closet. They have as much intelligence and brain power that they need to survive. Humans, by definition, have an average IQ of 100. While it may be impossible to measure, fish have been described as having IQ's between one and two. Surely we should be able to outsmart a fish most of the time? This book will help you do just that.

We know well that a fish is in its preferred habitat doing what it does each and every day. After a while if it doesn't get eaten by another fish, bird or mammal, it learns what it must do or not do to survive — and some fish get quite good at it. Remember, however, you are much, much smarter than a fish, so in most situations you should be able to hold your own! Good fly selection, a stealthy approach, a natural presentation and proper line control will set the stage for that moment of truth when the fish selects your fly as something it wants to eat. Oh yeah, Fish On!

Surely you have heard the phrase "you should have been here yesterday". Keep in mind that fish must eat sometime in order to survive. One skill we all need to work on is to arrive when the fish are actively feeding and looking for something more to eat. Often these opportunistic, even explosive, episodes are unpredictable but many times if we use our intelligence and some key information we might be able to improve the odds to our favor. Provoking a fish to take your fly is an exhilarating part of fly fishing. While the fish may be hooked, you are similarly hooked on the adrenalin rush of the moment.

Certainly the tips outlined in this book will help you become a better angler. Often the secret merely is to figure out what your targeted fish is naturally eating at the exact moment you are making a cast. While remaining undetected, if you present a fly that effectively mimics the natural prey in size, shape, color and behavior, you are well on your way to catching a lot of fish.

To help understand how a given fly works and to exploit it to our advantage, we need to know a few pertinent fish feeding behaviors. In this book, we explore some simple predator/prey relationships and in particular, speculate on what makes a fish actually want to eat your fly. After all, one of the reasons many of us go fly fishing is to catch a fish.

The author holds a pretty brook trout prior to release. Note that the camo waders aid in making stealthy approaches to wary fish.

Make no mistake, a fish is constantly aware of what is going on all around it and it is this awareness that helps it survive to another day. The moment that protective shield lapses, the fish becomes vulnerable to every predator including you — the angler. If you consider the broad daily swings in the Dow Jones Industrial Average as an indicator of stock market paranoia, you might get an inkling of why a fish behaves as it does: a fish wants to eat greedily yet not become a meal itself. A smart fish learns early on that it can't have it both ways!

To dramatize this point even further, fish have evolved many strategies for reproducing themselves. Some fish may spawn many thousands or millions of eggs over their lifetime while other fish produce eggs in more modest numbers. In the end though, only two offspring need to survive to adulthood from the two parent fish to achieve a stable population. The point here is that many dumb, naive or unsuspecting fish get eaten every day. As an angler, we love to find and catch these more vulnerable fish.

A beautiful brook trout in spawning colors.

While fish may not be as intelligent as a human, they do have some keen senses to help them from being eaten by some other animal. For example, we would expect fish to see quite well. Fish can see many shades between black and white and many species can also distinguish specific subtle color variations. Moreover, some scientists believe that fish also may be able to see light in the ultraviolet spectrum as well as react to reflected polarized light.

Fish respond to abrupt movement especially if the object moves differently from what they know to be safe. A tree moves, no problem; an animal or its shadow moves and the fish seeks immediate shelter. Just remember, **when a fish is in a defensive mode it is not going to eat.**

Fish have coloration patterns that help them blend in to their surroundings. Sometimes these patterns or shades change and often the angler might only see the shadow of a passing fish. On a sandy bonefish flat, the angler may have great difficulty trying to see a six-pound fish in two feet of water 25 feet away. Why? These fish have evolved a coloration scheme that allows them to move about and blend in. Most often, their moving shadow is the only clue that betrays their ghostly presence.

Fish can smell. They have keen olfactory sensors and react to some very subtle odors. The classic example is when an adult spawning salmon returns to its natal stream after being at sea for several years. Research has shown that it follows imprinted odors uniquely characteristic to its birthplace. The fidelity of a returning fish to a particular river is without doubt one of the wonders of nature.

Fish can hear well and, in fact, because sound travels five times faster and much farther in water than in air a fish may hear you coming from quite a distance. Always practice stealth when approaching your favorite fishing spot. Your mantra should be to "walk softly when carrying a long fly rod." Keep the noise down to whispers — and remember, stealth.

A fish's lateral line is a unique sensory organ not found in other animals. A network of nerve sensors is located on both sides of the fish from head to tail. Using the lateral line sensors, the fish can perceive sound patterns and pressure changes that might arise from a fish swimming nearby. The ability of a fish to swim in a highly coordinated formation found in some fish schools can be attributed primarily to external information it receives from its eyes and lateral line. A tight schooling pattern is critical for a prey species that uses schooling behavior and flash to confuse or avoid predators. Meanwhile, schooling predators feed more efficiently when they hunt in packs to concentrate prey species in tight groups. Survival for a fish is a continuous battle as the real world is dynamic and quite violent, especially if you are a little fish.

Larger fish will often use turbulence and chaotic water flows to take advantage of smaller fish that easily become momentarily disoriented. Understanding how to recognize and fish these dynamic habitats can often produce quality catches. Knowing what fly to use and how it should behave will without doubt enhance your angling success.

Tidal rips commonly attract feeding predators where they have an advantage over disoriented baitfish.

A fishing fly is not alive but is made to look so. If you are a fly tier, you apply your skills to dress a hook into an effective lure. In this impressionistic art form, you assemble fur, feathers, synthetics and thread to create something a fish wants to eat. Your action when selecting materials to tie the fly as well as angling techniques you use to make it appear natural is what distinguishes fly fishing from many other sports and what makes it appealing to an increasing number of people.

Angling with a fly is a contemplative sport where you can get some peace and quiet. At the very least, you often fish in beautiful places with the backdrop sounds of flowing water, singing birds and other natural rhythms. Certainly fly fishing will take you to new places as you explore new waters to fish. You will witness other wildlife including birds and mammals not commonly seen by other more hurried observers. Most important of all you will earn lifetime memories and build stronger friendships as you share experiences and stories with your fellow anglers.

Catching a fish using your guile and wit is a pleasurable experience. Breathing fresh air, laughing about the one that got away and getting some quality outdoor exercise are all known as positive health factors. It is also difficult to worry about your daily problems when you are concentrating on catching a fish. Clearly, fly fishing is an ideal stress reduction activity. With this perspective, my hope is that through fly fishing you will live a longer, more balanced and happier life.

CHAPTER

ONE

How to Select The Right Fly

Selecting the right fly can be as complicated or as simple as you wish to make it. Let's choose simple first and then, as you increase your experience in the sport, you can become more embroiled in the practice of fly selection. Remember, most good anglers catch most of their fish on about five or six flies — and they do so just about everyday they go fishing. Since I know you want to catch fish without much ado, let me outline a simple process that will get you oriented quickly as to what fly you might use today.

Let's begin by selecting the species of fish you might be seeking. According to the *National Survey of Fishing, Hunting and Outdoor Associated Recreation* recently published by the U. S. Fish and Wildlife Service, more than 3 million fly anglers over 16 years of age fished more than 30 million days in 2006. In addition to all the self-sustaining fish populations, the American Fisheries Society (Halverson, 2008) reports that in 2004, 1.75 billion fish weighing almost 45 million pounds were stocked in the United States. Rainbow trout, a favorite of coldwater fly anglers, are most often released at catchable sizes and account for more than 22 million pounds or about 50% of the total weight stocked.

Predictably, many freshwater fly anglers sought coldwater species of trout, salmon and steelhead. Largemouth and smallmouth bass, together known as black bass, make up another popular grouping. Panfish, including sunfish, rock bass, perch, walleye and crappie, are typical warmer water species popular with large numbers of anglers. In saltwater, the most popular species targeted by anglers include sea trout, drum, snook, stripped bass, bluefish, mahi-mahi and bonito. Moreover, even though some marine anglers may well have to go to warm tropical waters, many enjoy the shear power of a bonefish, tarpon or permit taken on a fly.

DAYS FISHED FOR EACH GROUPING

FISH	ANGLERS	DAYS FISHED
Panfish	16.5 million	200 million
Black Bass	10 million	420 million
Trout/Salmon	8 million	90 million
Coastal Predators	5.5 million	64 million

Source: *2006 National Survey of Fishing, Hunting and Outdoor Associated Recreation, US Fish and Wildlife Service.*

I acknowledge that I cannot include every possible fish species sought by fly anglers worldwide. The principles of what I outline here, however, should serve you well should you one day wish to target other species like peacock bass, rooster fish, mahi-mahi, and a host of other wonderful sport fish. Nevertheless, to keep things simple, we will use the following groups: **Panfish**, **Black Bass**, **Trout/Salmon** and **Coastal Predators**.

I have developed for you a flow diagram for each of these groups that will guide you. By answering three or four simple questions you can select the proper fly line and then the best fly. Here are the questions:

- **What do you want to catch?**
- **How fast is the water moving?**
- **Are the fish feeding at the surface?**
- **About how deep is the water?**

Once we have the species grouping clearly in mind, the next question is whether we are going to fish where the water is actively flowing as in a river, stream or tidal inlet or flat water like a placid bay, estuary, pond or lake. These two questions can be answered in the comfort of your easy chair back home.

The fly selection process, however, continues with a couple of key observations that you will have to make when you arrive waterside. The first observation involves signs of surface feeding. Do you see fish actively breaking the water's surface? Seabirds, like gulls and terns, diving in concentrated areas can be an effective indicator of fish feeding on the surface. In other less chaotic, though no less exciting scenarios, fish may be rhythmically feeding on something from the water's surface here and there. You may see and, quite often hear a violent burst as the fish rips its meal off the surface film. Sometimes the fish will come clear out of the water in a spectacular display of aggressive feeding behavior. At other times, the fish may merely sip an object from the surface and make only the slightest disturbance or ripple. Getting a clear understanding of these surface feeding expressions is suggestive of what type of fly you may want to tie on your line.

Hovering seabirds can often guide you to where predators are forcing bait-fish closer to the surface.

Conversely, should you arrive at your fishing spot and see or hear no fish activity, you have to assume that: 1) there are no fish there; or 2) the fish are there but you can't see them. If it's the latter, we come to our second observation, which is to make an approximate assessment of water depth. In order to get our fly down to where the fish may be feeding, we may have to switch our fly line from one that floats to one that partially sinks like a sink tip line or perhaps even a full sinking line.

Floating lines will generally be satisfactory for water depths less than five feet. In water between six feet and 15 feet, a sink tip fly line likely will be just fine. For deeper water, we would be better served if we used a full sink fly line. Be mindful of the advertised sink rate that should be displayed on the fly line packaging. For waters deeper than 15 feet especially if there is a strong current, we may want to get our fly down quickly to where the fish are feeding. Here we may want to use a fast sink fly line. Remember, you can always ask the fly fishing specialist at your local fly shop to help you select the proper fly line for any given situation. *See Sink Rate Table on facing page.*

Okay, we have made several decisions and taken several observations. For example, we know what fish we want to catch, we know if the water is flowing quickly or not, we are aware of obvious fish surface feeding and we have some idea of the depth of the water. Based on our analysis to this point, we have selected just the right fly line. How does all of this relate to which fly I need to catch a fish? Let's answer that question.

SINK RATES

Sink rates are commonly expressed in inches per second (I/S). While there is some variability in the way manufacturers describe the sink rates of their fly lines, they all use I/S. Nevertheless, if the water is slow and not too deep, a slower sink rate will generally satisfy your need to get the fly down to where the fish are feeding. Alternatively, if the water is deep and/or is moving quickly, you may decide to use a fly line with a faster sink rate. You estimate how deep your fly is by counting the number of seconds that passed since it hit the water.

Common Designation	Characteristic	Sink Rate (Inches/Second)
I or 1	Slow/Very Slow	1 - 2
II or 2	Medium Fast/Fast	2 - 3
III or 3	Fast/Extra Fast	3 - 4
IV or 4	Very Fast	4 - 5
V or 5/6	Fastest	5 - 7

Since so many fly anglers enjoy fishing for **TROUT**
and their close relatives salmon, I will start with that
group. Below is our first flow diagram.

TROUT

**How fast
is the
water moving?**

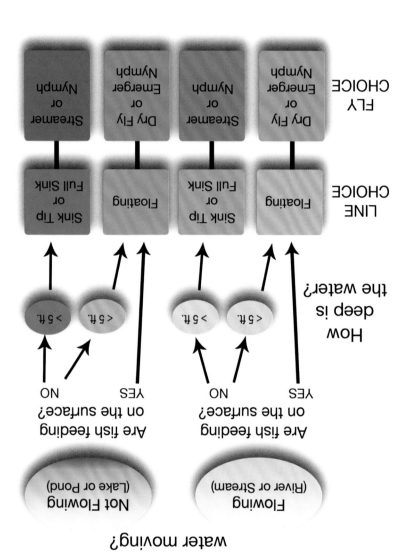

Flowing
(River or Stream)

Not Flowing
(Lake or Pond)

**Are fish feeding
on the surface?**

YES   NO

**Are fish feeding
on the surface?**

YES   NO

**How
deep is
the water?**

> 5 ft.   < 5 ft.

> 5 ft.   < 5 ft.

LINE CHOICE

Floating

Sink Tip
or
Full Sink

Floating

Sink Tip
or
Full Sink

FLY CHOICE

Dry Fly
or
Emerger
Nymph

Nymph

Streamer
or
Nymph

Dry Fly
or
Emerger
Nymph

Streamer
or
Nymph

By following the flow chart, you see that we have four outcomes of which two are unique. Essentially, if we use a floating line, we will want to use a **dry fly,** an **emerger or a nymph**. On the other hand, if we are using a sink tip or full sink fly line, we will want to use a **streamer or nymph.**

For **TROUT** here are the flies for each group.

DRY FLY

Adams
Black Gnat Parachute
Elk Hair Caddis
Ant
Grasshopper
Blue Wing Olive
Stimulator
Royal Wulff
Humpy

EMERGER

CDC Emerger
The Usual

STREAMER

Woolly Bugger
Mickey Finn
Muddler Minnow
Hornberg

NYMPH

Bead Head Hare's Mask Nymph
Pheasant Tail Nymph
Prince Nymph
Copper John
Soft Hackle

There you have them. These are 20 really great flies for trout. I would venture to say that a vast majority of trout caught by fly anglers throughout the world are caught with the patterns on the above list. If you are going to fish for trout, don't leave home without them.

Rainbow trout takes a Woolly Bugger.

Later, I will describe each fly and guide you on how to select which to use first. Most importantly, you will learn how to make your fly behave as if it were natural fish food.

Now that we have a handle on trout, let's take a look at another group of popular fish to catch. Few can doubt that **BLACK BASS** (primarily largemouth and smallmouth bass) are a jewel of American anglers.

In 2006, more than 10 million black bass anglers fished 420 million days. Comparatively, about 8 million trout and salmon anglers fished almost 90 million days. Black bass can be a great thrill to catch on a fly rod and when many of the above baitcast and spin anglers find out about fly fishing, they will be in for a great threat.

Rock Bass, another variety of black bass.

Large-mouth Bass. This lunker black-bass was caught on a Hornberg Streamer.

BLACKBASS

LARGEMOUTH BASS, SMALLMOUTH BASS

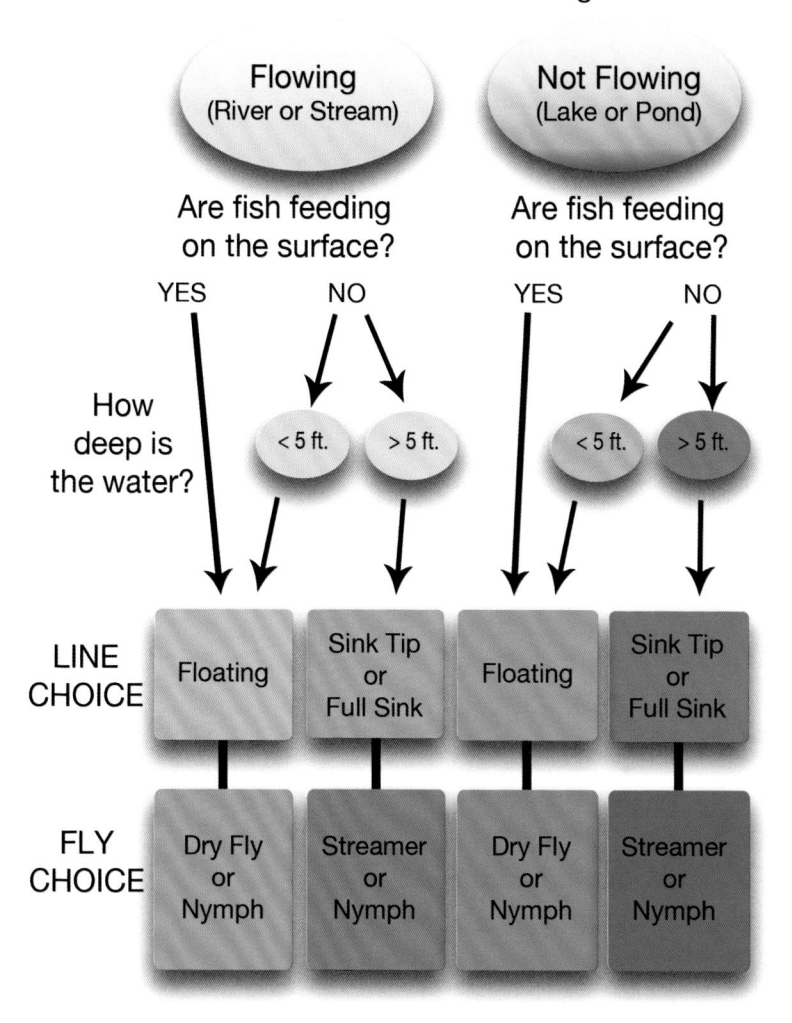

Again by following the flow chart, you see that we have four outcomes of which two are unique. Essentially, if we use a floating line, we will want to use a **dry fly, popper or nymph.** On the other hand, if we are using a sink tip or full sink fly line, we will want to use a **streamer** or **nymph**.

For **BLACK BASS**, here are the blue ribbon flies for each fly choice group.

DRY FLY

Adams
Black Gnat Parachute
Elk Hair Caddis
Grasshopper
Blue Wing Olive
Bob's Banger (popper)
Stimulator
Royal Wulff

STREAMER

Clouser Deep Minnow
Deceiver
Woolly Bugger
Mickey Finn
Muddler Minnow
Hornberg

NYMPH

Bead Head Hare's Mask Nymph
Pheasant Tail Nymph
Prince Nymph
Copper John
Soft Hackle Fly

Bluegill, the most commonly caught panfish.

Black Crappie, a common panfish.

Our third group of fish is immensely popular with American anglers. In 2006, 16.5 million anglers fished over 200 million days for **PAN FISH** including bluegill, crappie, perch and walleye. What makes these numbers even more remarkable is that they don't include the Great Lakes fishery nor the many millions of youngsters under 16 years of age. Most angler's first fish was probably a bluegill!

PAN FISH
BLUEGILL, PERCH, CRAPPIE, WALLEYE

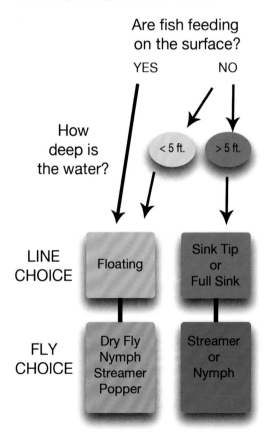

Here we use one less question because as we fish for **Pan Fish** we are less concerned about water flow. In most cases, we will be fishing in lakes and ponds where the water flow is minimal. Again, as we follow the flow chart, we see that there are two unique outcomes. Essentially, if we use a floating line, we will want to use a **dry fly, nymph**, **streamer** or **popper**. On the other hand, if we are using a sink tip or full sink fly line, we will want to use a **streamer** or **nymph**.

For **PAN FISH**, here are the flies for each group.

DRY FLY
Adams
Black Gnat Parachute
Elk Hair Caddis
Ant
Grasshopper
Blue Wing Olive
Bob's Banger (popper)
Stimulator
Humpy
Royal Wulff

STREAMER
Woolly Bugger
Mickey Finn
Muddler Minnow
Clouser Minnow
Deceiver
Hornberg

NYMPH
Bead Head Hare's Mask Nymph
Pheasant Tail Nymph
Prince Nymph
Copper John
Soft Hackle Fly

Yellow Perch caught on a Bead Head Hare's Mask Nymph.

Our last group of fish is **COASTAL PREDATORS**. In 2006, more than 5.5 million saltwater anglers fished over 64 million days for striped bass, bluefish, drum, sea trout and other coastal species. Catching any of these fish on a fly rod is a real thrill because they are powerful critters that can provide a strenuous battle to even the most seasoned angler.

Coastal Predators

Striped Bass, Bluefish, Sea Trout, Redfish, Bonefish, Bonito

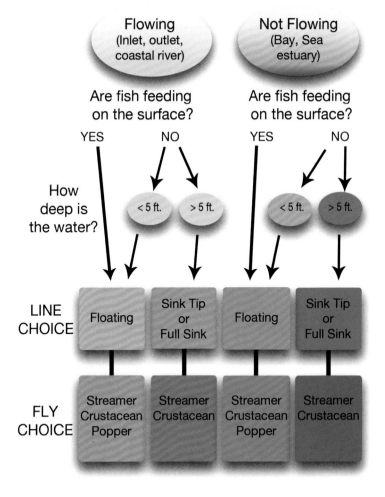

Our flow chart guide offers three types of flies: Streamers, crustaceans and poppers.

For **COASTAL PREDATORS**, the flies for each fly choice group are listed below.

STREAMERS
Clouser Deep Minnow
Deceiver
Woolly Bugger
Mickey Finn

CRUSTACEANS
Crazy Charlie

POPPER
Bob's Banger

That's it! It is really that simple. Now, if you look back over the list of flies recommended for each group of fish, you will notice a great overlap. The point is that most predators, freshwater or saltwater, will feed on about the same things. For example, a **Woolly Bugger** that will entice a fish in freshwater will be an effective fly in saltwater as well. In saltwater where the quarry may be quite big, the **bugger** you use will be tied on larger size rust resistant hooks. In freshwater the fish may believe it to be a leech while in saltwater it may be more of an eel or sea worm imitation. Nevertheless, I am convinced that a **Woolly Bugger** will catch fish wherever predators swim.

So, if you are anxious to get out fishing right now, get some of the recommended flies and have at it. They'll work! Still, if you want to improve your chances of catching a lot of fish, read on. I have a lot more information to boost your knowledge and even more understanding of these most effective flies. For example, we have yet to discuss critical fish behaviors and how it might relate to your fly. Also, you need to ensure that you are using equipment that is balanced, that you understand where the fish are likely to be and that you really know how to set the hook at the moment of truth when the fish mouths your fly. I use the rest of the book to lay out this information for you.

Barracuda, a predator of the tidal flats, takes a Crazy Charlie fly.

A large mahi-mahi, a coastal predator.

CHAPTER

TWO

OTHER FLY SELECTION FACTORS

O kay, here you are out on the water and fishing away. Foremost, you are having fun and if only you would catch a fish or two, it would be that much better. Now at least we have a short list of well-proven flies that have over many years taken lots of fish for lots of fly anglers. You have answered the questions, followed the flow chart, have the proper fly line so your next question most likely will be: which of these flies should I use first? Let's take a moment to look at a few more factors that might influence and guide your decision.

Factors you might use to select a fly:

1 ⟿ Fly "matches the hatch" or comes very close (same size, shape and color) to what the fish may be eating at the moment.

I have said in the past that the game of fly fishing is to figure out the daily puzzle of what the fish are eating. Fish do change their diets and sometimes that change can occur in a matter of minutes. Sometimes it can be over days or weeks or months. Trying to keep up with what the fish are feeding on at the moment is why hiring a guide might help you orient more quickly to a new water. Good guides are out there with the fish everyday and as such, understand better the pulses and rhythms associated with their home waters. Still, there are those of us who like to go it alone.

We like to figure it out for ourselves no matter how long it takes. Perhaps we are too stubborn or cheap. Perhaps we are gluttons for punishment. Perhaps we just enjoy the pasttime of fishing and the beauty that surrounds us. Nonetheless, on most fishing trips, it usually is more fun to catch a fish so here is some advice.

The first thing you do as you approach any water that you plan to fish is to watch for fish activity. A swirl here, a rise there, birds chasing baitfish — look for any sign that might indicate feeding fish. If there are fish moving about taking food off the surface, look very closely for what they may be feeding on. Really try to figure it out. Is it a bug? A small fish? A mulberry? Sometimes selective fish will be focused on one prey species and probably for reasons of efficiency and safety, they will feed exclusively or nearly so on that prey.

If you see small fish or insects darting about, try to capture one. Absent an outright capture, can you distinguish its size, shape or color? Keep trying to find out as much as you can. Even if you can get one of the three, size for example, tie on a fly that is about the same size and begin to fish. Meanwhile use your senses to tune in to what is going on about you. Each clue will help guide you toward better fly selection. If you are fortunate to catch a fish, a harmless stomach pump procedure can extract previously eaten prey to help you conduct an on the spot analysis. Each bit of information should help you refine your fly selection to most approximate a reasonable match of the fish's current diet. When you solve this puzzle, you are in the best position to catch fish — sometimes a lot of them!

2 — You just caught a fish on that fly and decide to continue to fish it.

Success often breeds success! If you get a fly that works and catches fish, stick with it as long as you like. Sometimes I get in a groove (others may call it a lull)

where I catch a few fish and am just content. I don't feel
like (perhaps I am too lazy) taking the time to change flies.
But hey, I am catching some fish and I am having fun so
who cares, this isn't necessarily a competitive sport is it?

The point is that if the fly you are currently using
catches fish, you must be in the ball park. If you do
change flies, not only will you loose precious fishing time,
you might switch to something that is less productive.
One strategy is to continue using this fly until you get
additional information that suggests that another pattern
might be more effective. In other words: base your change
on solid information.

3 ⤳ You have a lot of confidence in fishing that pattern. Perhaps you've used the same fly on these waters in the past.

As I arrive at the water's edge and scan about looking
for signs of fish feeding activity, I may initially see
nothing that suggests why I might use a particular pattern.
In these cases, I might very well select a fly because it
is one of my favorite "**search patterns**." I know it has
worked before, perhaps on these very same waters, so why
wouldn't it work now? You see, I have a lot of confidence
in this fly and I know how to fish it. So I tie it on and
start to fish keeping alert to any hint that might make me
change my mind and tie on something else.

So while awaiting more data to compel me to change
the pattern, I will continue to fish my favorite. I will
use the same fishing strategies to make that fly appear
to be a natural prey species, meaning that I will do my
best to make it behave just as a natural would. Perhaps I
might even try to make it look a bit infirmed or wounded
— anything to suggest to the predator that my fly is
debilitated or that it is real and natural food. I want the
fish to believe that taking my fly is as easy as going to a
Sunday picnic in the park!

4 — A fellow angler suggests using a pattern that recently caught fish in this location.

I was fishing in a river recently and a fellow came up to me and offered a suggested fly pattern. He said he had been fishing there almost daily and had been doing quite well. I told him what I was using: one of my favorite dry flies — a **Black Gnat Parachute** — and he noted that while that pattern might work, his pattern (a **Blue Wing Olive**) was more of a certainty. I thanked him for his advice and continued to fish my pattern. There was no visible or predominant hatch going on, so why change.

After a while, I still didn't raise one fish so I moved about the pool still remaining with my original fly. Time continue to pass and still no fish. I figured I had to do something so I started changing patterns more regularly. Still nothing. I even tried his suggested pattern and my bad luck continued. Giving up on that pool, I then went downstream and began fishing a favorite nymph pattern and started to catch a few fish.

The point is that while someone may offer a suggested pattern to you, it may or may not improve your catch rate. If you are not catching anything with the fly you are using, consider changing to the suggested pattern if you have that fly in your inventory. If it works, that's great. If not, at least you can eliminate that pattern for the moment and try something else.

5 — The fly is a known attractor pattern on the waters you are fishing.

Attractor patterns have the ability to catch fish when no other flies seem to work. One characteristic of an attractor pattern is that it may not necessarily look like anything naturally available in the waters you are fishing. What makes these types of patterns stir the interest of a fish is a matter of speculation. Perhaps it has a color, silhouette or shape that makes it too compelling to resist. Perhaps it is how it sits or flows through the water that suggests to a fish that it is a food opportunity that is just not to be missed. The Humpy, Royal Wulff and Copper John are good examples of attractor patterns.

Royal Wulff on left and a Humpy on the right are attractor patterns. Give them a try when no other flies seem to work.

   One thing you might consider when you will be fishing in new waters is to stop by the local tackle or fly shop and ask about flies that have been working lately. Ask specifically if there are any attractor patterns that should be considered. Note recommended sizes and ask if there are any special techniques or tricks on how to fish them. As a gesture of thanks to the store owner for this valuable information, you might even consider purchasing a Royal Wulff on left and a Humpy on the right, and a few of these recommended flies and take them along. If the opportunity presents itself and you have no clue as to what the fish may be eating, tie on one of your new flies and see what happens. With a bit of luck, a fish may take your fly and start you on a day of great fishing.

6 —꙾ You have a hunch that the fly just looks so natural, so why not.

   There are a few flies in my fly box that just look so

buggy or natural that they seem, at least to me, to be irresistible. They have color, texture, bristles and shape that would suggest that they are real. When under water, they move and appear to undulate as if they were alive. If it appears to be alive, surely a feeding fish will take interest and accept it as its next meal.

High among these are my **Hare's Mask** and **Pheasant Tail nymphs.** I like to use either of these patterns to probe likely waters when there is no surface activity to suggest top-feeding fish are about. Sometimes you just have to play your hunch that a specific fly might work.

If you deliver it to the most likely **holding areas**, allow it to drift drag free, and maintain good line control between you and the fly, you surely will be rewarded with a take. Having confidence and a positive attitude when fishing a fly can be a great asset. If you think it might work, it very well might!

7 — You purchased or tied this fly specifically for this trip.

There are some waters that have very predictable hatches and favored fly patterns. There may be articles written or websites available that clearly outline the flies you must bring along with you if you intend to fish in these waters during the specific periods noted.

Taking this information, you purchase or tie a series of these special flies specifically for this trip. Now as you get out on the water, you follow through by tying on one of these custom-tied beauties.

If the pattern information you got was reliable and not hyped by some overzealous outdoor writer, you may very well have a chance to catch a lot of fish. Certainly you were prepared and did your homework. I'll give you three cheers for effort!

8 ⤳ After giving the fly a fair chance to work, you decide to change to another pattern.

A common question is: "how often should I change my fly?" While this is a very simple question, the answer is far more complex. Let me give you some examples. There are times when I fish the same fly all day. Perhaps I am confident in the ultimate outcome or maybe I'm just too lazy to change the fly. Often, I will just move a few steps and try it again in another likely fish holding spot.

Nevertheless, if I am in a good fishing spot and confident that there are fish lurking nearby, I will be patient and might change to another fly pattern after 15-30 minutes. Meanwhile, I am searching for any visual indicators like an obvious insect hatch or fish feeding at or near the surface. I am really tuned in and trying hard to figure out any active feeding going on right in front of me. If I am sure that the fish are seeing my fly and turning their nose to it, I might make a change to yet another pattern after five or six casts.

Another idea that I use occasionally is to fish with a pal with each of us using a different pattern. Sharing information between two or more anglers is fun and sometimes helps to quickly determine the successful fly.

Probably the best answer I can give you on when to change a fly is when you are no longer confident that you will achieve your intended outcome with your current fly. Going back to the investment metaphor, do you want to be an investor (and change less often) or a trader (and change with every new observation you make)? Both can lead to success and catching fish. Remember though, each time you stop to change flies, your hook is not in the water; and as my grandfather told me long ago, your fly has to be in the water in order to catch a fish.

Some guides suggest using dark patterns on dark days and bright flies in clear, sunny weather. Perhaps there is some wisdom to this rule of thumb, but it is not something

I dwell upon particularly. When I want to use my chartreuse and white **Clouser Minnow**, this is what I will start with regardless of cloud cover. If this fly zeros out after a reasonable chance, then I might consider making a change — perhaps to a lighter or darker fly.

9 ⟶ **Even though your fly seems to match the hatch, you decide to use a fly slightly bigger or smaller in the same pattern.**

While a size 12 Bead Head Hare's Mask Nymph is generally recommended for most fishing opportunities, an angler may wish to add a few additional sizes for those times when fish are being more selective. This photo depicts the same nymph (l to r) in Size 10, 12, 14 and 18.

There are times when you encounter a massive hatch. Millions of bugs are on the water and the fish are going nuts. You believe that you are in luck as you have the exact match. You tie it onto your tippet and make your first cast. Nothing. You are persistent and try again, and yet again. Nothing. The fish are rising all about you; what is going wrong? Perhaps your fly looks so much like every other natural out there that it gets lost and there is nothing to distinguish it from the rest.

Rather than calling it a day and going home, there may be a couple of things you might do when you are fishing in the midst of a massive hatch. The first place to start is to try to make your fly appear to be slightly different. You might tie on a pattern that is slightly larger than the naturals. Here, at least, your fly may appear to be larger. Next, you might make it move slower or faster than what the naturals are doing. If neither of these strategies work, you could tie on a fly pattern that looks totally different than the naturals. One suggestion might be to try an attractor fly or perhaps a streamer. The first will appear very different and the later would have underwater movement that might provoke a strike. Make no mistake about it; fishing among millions of naturals is extremely difficult yet if you are persistent, you may well be rewarded with a hook up or two.

Bead Head Flies:
Hare's Ear,
Pheasant Tail
and Prince.

Most nymph patterns can be tied with a bead to give added weight to the head of the fly. To use a bead or not is usually determined by water depth or current speed. Usually in faster or deep water, I will choose a bead head to help me get my fly down to where I believe the fish maybe holding.

10—⌒ The fly can get to the desired depth where the fish are most likely feeding.

When the fish are not feeding on the surface, you may have to get your fly down to a depth where the fish are likely to see it. In addition to using weighted flies, fly anglers have another advantage over bait and lure anglers and that is we can switch our fly line quickly from one that floats to one that sinks.

So when do you select and use a sinking, sinking tip, or floating fly line? This decision is dictated on where you believe the fish are going to be. When I'm fishing shallow areas (less than 5 feet deep) like small rivers, streams, ponds or salt flats, typically I am using a 9-foot leader. Here, a floating fly line works great. Whether you are fishing a wet fly (it sinks) or a dry fly (it floats), the fly line will have minimal influence on the fly's ability to get to a depth or float as it was designed to do.

When using wet flies and the depth of the water increases beyond five feet, you will find increasing satisfaction going to a sinking tip fly line and then to a full sink line if you really want to get your fly down quickly to much deeper waters. Sinking fly lines have variable sink rates so if you need to get deep in a hurry, use one with a higher grain weight designation.

I certainly hope the above discussion brings you closer to an understanding of how you might select just the right fly for the day you are out on your favorite waters. If you are still undecided, perhaps the next chapter, where we look at each pattern in more detail, might help you narrow your selection to that one fly that will be so compelling that fish can't resist striking it!

CHAPTER

THREE

THE 24 GREATEST FLIES

In this chapter we will discuss each of the recommended fly patterns and offer some insight on why they were selected for my special list. I think you will see a trend that each of these fantastic flies is time-tested and has a strong record of catching fish. While I encourage you to learn how to tie these flies, I realize that fly tying may have to wait until a later time. Meanwhile, these flies are generally available and your local fly shop should have them or should be able to order them for you. Purchasing your flies locally offers the advantage, in addition to the fishing suggestions I might offer, for you to learn local fishing techniques from fellow fly anglers who may have considerable experience using these same flies. Now, let's look at each fly.

SIX GREAT DRY FLIES

Grasshopper

Blue Wing Olive

Adams

Black Gnat Parachute

Elk Hair Caddis

Ant

Dry flies float on or above the water's surface and are meant to be fished with a floating fly line. If your line sinks, it will drag the fly underwater. Except where noted, fish your dry flies high on the surface, meaning the fly should sit high, held by the water's surface tension.

1 —⸰Adams

The **Adams** is very likely every angler's favorite dry fly. Richard Talleur in his book *Mastering the Art of Fly-Tying* says that it is hard to beat an **Adams** as any angler's life long fly pattern. With its gray body, brown and gray hackle and striated wings, it mimics very well many insects. In or out of the water, this pattern is just a beautiful fly.

A true generalist's fly, some anglers believe it to mimic a flying ant; others believe it might suggest a caddis and still others, myself included, use it to imitate several species of mayfly. I have never met a good angler who didn't have at least one **Adams**. It looks great, it looks buggy and it looks edible and I think that the fish you seek will agree.

This classic American dry fly is generally attributed to Leonard Halladay who lived near Mayfield Pond in Michigan. Back in 1922, he tied the first one upon the request of Charles Adams. Adams was on a fishing trip and wanted to replicate an insect he saw earlier in the day. He described it to Halladay and the rest is history.

Today, there are many slight variations of the **Adams**, my favorite being the **Parachute Adams** (built with a dorsal post similar to the **Black Gnat Parachute** described below) which I believe is equally effective.

The best way to fish this fly is to let it float high on the water's surface, being held up by the water's own surface tension. As with most dry flies, it is a good idea to treat this fly with dry fly floatant before it gets wet. When drag sets in at the end of a drag-free downstream drift, simply lift the fly from the water and recast it to another fish holding spot.

2—Black Gnat Parachute

When I'm fishing for trout and the going gets tough and all else fails, I bring out my "go-to" fly. I have caught more fish on this dry fly than all other dry flies. Perhaps it is because there are so many black bugs out there in the wild that this fly looks natural. I mostly like to fish it high on the water so I will press a fair amount of dry fly floatant (I like Scientific Anglers the best), a silicon like gel, into it's fibers before I begin to fish it.

After you catch one or two fish on it, the fly often

becomes slimed and a high float becomes impossible. Even multiple false casts won't get the fly adequately dry. At this point, I need to wash the fly and then press it against my shirt sleeve to rid it of excess water. Another application of the dry fly floatant and I am ready to go.

If you look closely at any parachute fly, you will notice a post on the upper side. When I tie this pattern, I bring the residual (butt end) tail fibers forward and integrate them into the post to stabilize it and also to give it additional strength. I usually use hollow white caribou hair as a post, but any light-weight hair or poly fiber would work almost as well. Sometimes making your post with contrasting colors like fluorescent orange, yellow, or red will allow you to see your fly more easily as it floats downstream. This trick can be especially helpful when the water's surface is filled with many floating white bubbles.

Wrapped around the post is a small feather or two. The bristles from these feathers radiate outward from the post. When you cast the fly and as it descends to the water's surface, the bristles give the fly additional drag much like a falling parachute; the weight of the hook always makes the fly land upright.

My preferred way of fishing the fly on still water is to cast it out and let it sit still for a moment. I might even slowly count to ten. At that point, I give it a slight twitch by stripping the fly line an inch or two. If you have ever seen a real fly hit the water, it often sits there stunned for a few seconds before it starts to struggle. I might even repeat the rest/strip sequence a few more times before I lift and cast elsewhere.

Even then, the initial draw of the fly off the water should begin slowly and then increase speed to a full casting movement. I can remember several times when a fish would rise to the fly when it was in the slow phase of the draw. Perhaps the fish was reacting to a skittering bug trying to break from the surface and become airborne. The slow initial draw of any dry fly also has an additional benefit of eliminating the loud air bubble pop surely to scare any fish within 20 feet.

When fishing in flowing water, the visible post really comes in handy to help you locate where the fly is during its downstream float. At the completion of the float, the fly can be lifted from the water and recast upstream. It can also be allowed to drag across the stream until it is directly downstream from the angler. At this point, the rod tip is lowered to the water as the fly is dragged underwater by the current. By slowly stripping the fly upstream back to you, you are fishing the fly like a submerged emerger. It is amazing how many extra fish I take using the upstream strip technique with this versatile fly. For trout or panfish, this pattern will catch fish for you.

3 ⌐ Elk Hair Caddis

This is another gem of a fly that is sure to catch some fish for you. This pattern is generally attributed to Al Troth and, for a dry fly, is easy to tie. Throughout the world, caddis flies are certain to be found wherever there are fish swimming — and fish love to eat caddis flies!

I like to tie them using a tan body and a rich brown hackle in hook sizes 12 -18, with my all-around favorite for all my dry flies being size 14. Other successful body color variations include olive, gray, yellow and even black. The wing can be light tan to dark chocolate brown.

When you get out on the river or lake and you see some bug skittering quickly about the surface, you are most likely seeing a caddis. Study this insect behavior carefully and try to get your fly to do the same thing. It helps using that dry fly floatant beforehand to keep the fly high and dry. By either moving the rod tip or stripping the fly line back toward you, the fly can be dragged across the water's surface similar to the way a natural insect might. Fish are aware of this behavior and commonly will pursue your skittering fly before it escapes, becomes airborne, or another fish takes it as a meal.

4—Ant

When the summer breezes blow, break out your **Ant** flies. Even more than caddis flies, ants occur throughout the world. Ant species number in the thousands. With this many ants scampering around doing what ants do, some of them are likely to fall into the water. On windy days, fish learn that the water's surface commonly will offer these tasty morsels as they are knocked off blades of riparian grass, over-hanging tree branches or falling leaves. In the summer and fall, fish eat a lot of ants.

From tiny to large, you will find ants in just about every color including black, red, and cinnamon to name a few, so your observations waterside will be critical to getting the best match. For me, it is just hard to beat the plain old black carpenter ant in size 14. Trout and panfish love them, and it doesn't seem to make too much of a difference whether you are fishing in flowing or non-flowing water.

5 — Grasshopper

If you think fish love ants for dinner, grasshoppers are an after-dinner delight. They are big and have lots of calories just as a dessert might. When conditions are right like in late summer and early fall when breezes blow and grasshoppers abound, fish await the awkward splash of a wayward grasshopper. Hoppers don't like water much and they certainly don't like to swim. A struggling grasshopper is as clear a signal for a fish as the clang of an iron triangle is to alert ranch hands that dinner is ready.

These are big flies, so a shorter (7-foot) 3X leader functions to deliver your fly very well. Finer tippets will generally twist in the wind and become knotted. A delicate presentation is not necessary. When the fly lands on the water, you might try and let it sit quietly for a moment. Next, strip the fly line a bit to make it twitch a couple of times. Usually that is all that is needed. If there is a nearby fish, particularly one that hasn't been caught recently by other anglers, it won't be able to resist.

There are many hopper patterns available. I like **Joe's Hopper** or **Dave's Hopper**. Either of these hopper patterns will work exceptionally well. Hoppers are great for trout, bass and many panfish.

6—Blue Wing Olive

An adaptation of an old world trout fly, this pattern has been altered by numerous fly tiers to adapt to local hatches of small mayflies. Usually tied on 18-22 hooks, with the higher number being smaller, this fly can be effective from April to November up north and perhaps even longer further south. Typically, this tiny fly has blue-gray wings, two long crystalline tail fibers and an olive green body. It can be tied with a split wing or as a parachute. Both types work.

Because you are using a smaller fly, you should also use a finer tippet material — perhaps 6X to 8X. These lighter tippets can be more difficult to work with, especially when tying attachment knots. Often, good light, a clean set of eyeglasses and patience will solve the problem for you.

Some anglers even tie several flies to 24-inch lengths of tippet at home. When they are on the river and need to change flies, they merely take one out and loop connect it to another loop tied at the residual end of their tapered leader.

The **Blue Wing Olive** is sometimes referred to as simply BWO. It must be fished without any surface drag whatsoever. On clear slow moving water, you might even want to add a wetting agent to the last few inches of your tippet to allow it to sink a bit. If a selective trout sees the leader floating on the surface film, it may well reject your fly.

FOUR GREAT NYMPH FLIES

Soft Hackle Fly, Copper John Nymph, Pheasant Tail Nymph & Bead Head Hare's Mask Nymph

Nymphs are a group of wet flies emulating aquatic insects that are designed to be fished beneath the water's surface. You can use a floating fly line in shallow water but for waters deeper than five feet, you will more likely have better success with a sinking tip or even a full sink line in water deeper than 15 feet.

7 Bead Head Hare's Mask Nymph

I mentioned earlier that I had another work-horse nymph and this is it. I think if I had only one nymph to take in my survival kit, it would be this fly. It is so effective on panfish, smallmouth bass as well as trout. I also like that this is a durable fly. I once caught more than 70 fish on one before an errant backcast lost it in some streamside alders. Nevertheless, when I am on a distant fishing trip like Alaska, I usually take two or three dozen with me. Sizes 10 through 18 are all effective, although, if I had to choose just one, I would select size 12. You really can't have enough flies of this pattern (also called a hare's ear nymph); if nothing more, you can give a few to your fishing pals and see them enjoy catching a few fish. They will appreciate the gesture!

I use a brass bead just behind the hook eye. The gold bead probably serves as a shiny attractor and provides the added weight to get the fly into the strike zone. There are many aquatic insects throughout the world and this fly evidently suggests to the fish some of the more edible ones like caddis, stoneflies, and mayflies. I've used it with considerable success in New Zealand, Argentina and all over North America.

As with all nymphs, you need to have great line control

to detect the slightest nibble. I don't like to use strike indicators (small floating line attachments equivalent to a bobber) because I believe they offer no advantage to an angler who maintains impeccable contact between the rod and the fly. When the nymph passes downstream in a drag free drift and even when it lifts or rises from the bottom at the end of the drift, this fly continues to fish. You never quite know when a fish will hit it, but hits you'll get.

8—Pheasant Tail Nymph

The **Pheasant Tail Nymph** is generally attributed to British River Keeper, Frank Sawyer.   Most modern adaptations are close approximations of his fly. Nevertheless, this is the second of my two work horse nymph flies.

Most anglers use it to simulate a swimming mayfly nymph. I usually tie it in size 14 although size 16 and 18 occasionally come in handy. I like it tied in with a small black tungsten or brass bead just behind the hook eye. When tied with the weight forward like this, it can appear to be swimming by merely making short fly line strips or perhaps raising or lowering the fly rod tip just a bit.

The fly, while effective at all depths, is best fished closer to the surface as it more closely resembles a swimming nymph. I also fish it in ponds and lakes for trout, perch, bluegill and crappie. When you see mayflies flying about but no surface rises, tie on a Pheasant Tail and be prepared to set your hook. The fish are likely taking the swimming nymphs before they can reach the surface. Getting your fly out there in the mix where it appears to be swimming about is sure to provoke a strike.

9—Copper John Nymph

John Barr of Boulder, Colorado, is best known as the originator of the **Copper John** nymph. Barr wanted a fly to sink quickly and integrated sequential copper wire wraps to suggest a segmented abdomen. His persistence resulted in this very successful design. Like the other two nymphs described above, this pattern is effective on trout, panfish and black bass. Jeff Fryhover of Umpqua Feather Merchants, a national fly supplier, told me that the **Copper John** was his most popular nymph.

When fishing in flowing water like a river or stream, be sure to eliminate drag or unnatural movement as the fly drifts downstream. You want the fly to move at the same rate as the water flow. Because the fly is weighted, it is likely to hug at or near the bottom. When it reaches its full downstream drift, it will begin to ascend from the bottom while moving back to your side of the river. This movement is not so unlike a nymph naturally emerging toward the surface. If you haven't caught it already, a fish following the drift will likely strike just as the fly begins to rise — so be ready. Since the fly line will already be somewhat taught, line control will not be a factor and setting the hook will almost be assured. This is the reason why many anglers catch fish on the rise and not on the drift. Fish will often mouth your fly imperceptibly during the drift and if you don't have good line control, you will never know it. If you can't see or feel the hit, you can't set the hook.

10—Soft Hackle Fly

This fly, or really a group of flies, goes all the way back to the history of fly tying where Dame Burner almost certainly used a variation of this pattern to catch fish for the Abbey's table. Sylvester Nemes, in his book, *Two Centuries of Soft Hackled Flies* also reviews the history and importance of this old world pattern. It is still around today because it remains an effective fish-catching class of flies.

On this fly, some feathers have stiff bristles or filaments that originate from a central spine. On other feathers, there seems to be less structure in the side filaments and therefore become more fluid-like, especially underwater. There are many feathers, including those from numerous game birds like quail, grouse and turkey that can be used for soft hackle flies but most come from domestic hens bread for this purpose. Color diversity, including striations and other natural patterns, abound.

Relatively simple to tie, the fly generally has a body made of natural or man-made fibers having mostly earth tone shades of brown, tan, gray, yellow, black or olive. Just behind the hook eye, a soft hackle feather is rotated two or three times around the hook shank to allow the feather's fibers to radiate outward. Tied off, that's it.

This is a great generalist fly because it can suggest lots of aquatic organisms. As with streamers, perhaps the best way to fish it is to allow it to sink and then have it slowly drift downstream with the current. The size of the fly (I like size 12 or 14), and the color (try gray, tan or olive) in combination with the undulating soft feather filaments fluttering in the current probably suggest to the fish leg or pre-emergent wing movements. The trick of all good fly anglers is to create in their fly the appearance of life where there is none.

SEVEN GREAT STREAMER FLIES

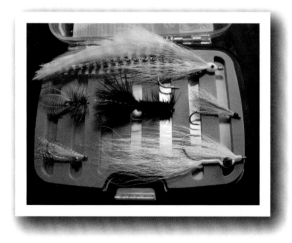

Deceiver, Hornberg, Woolly Bugger, Mickey Finn, Crazy Charlie, Clouser Minnow & Muddler Minnow.

Streamers are a group of flies that represent critters that swim. Most suggest prey species of fish while patterns exist for leeches, newts, tadpoles, crabs, shrimp and squid. Fish want to, indeed have to, eat. The action of a prey swimming, particularly something smaller and moving across or away from a predator, is quite compelling. Streamers were designed to provoke a primordial reflex to eat. Let's talk about some really fantastic streamer fly patterns.

11 ⟿ Woolly Bugger

Arguably, this pattern and its many derivatives, catch more fish than all other fly patterns combined. It is such a popular fly that there is a variant **Woolly Bugger** that will catch every possible recreational fish species including carp.

The **Woolly Bugger** itself evolved from an old English pattern, the **Woolly Worm**, and was tied by Charles Cotton in 1676. Russell Blessing of Harrisburg, Pennsylvania came up with the **bugger** design during the summer of 1967 as he tried to develop a pattern to emulate a hellgrammite or dobsonfly larvae. He merely substituted the yarn tail on the **Worm** pattern with a longer tail of black marabou. When wet, the feathery tail of marabou undulates and reflects light not so unlike the swimming tail of so many aquatic creatures. Blessing and his angling buddies were astonished at the initial success of his creation. Today, unless you are a dry fly purist, you simply must have some **Woolly Buggers** in your fly box — wherever you fish!

As wild as it may seem, author Gary Soucie devoted a whole book, *Woolly Wisdom,* to this one pattern and its 400 plus variations. For many of us who tie our own flies, this is most likely the first fly we learn to make. We teachers do this because the hook dressing principles you need to tie the **Woolly Bugger** are the same skills you will need to tie more complicated flies later on. In other words, if you can tie a good **Bugger**, you certainly will be able to, with practice, tie more advanced patterns. Even if you prove me wrong and never learn another pattern, you still will have tied an absolute killer fly!

Most **Woolly Bugger** flies are weighted and are designed to be fished below the surface. Fly tiers use metal wire, usually lead although a non-toxic tin alloy is now available, underneath the chenille body covering to ensure that the fly will sink quickly. Today, others use brass or tungsten beads, cone heads, and even small metal dumbbell eyes to add weight. For faster currents and deeper waters, some anglers combine the metal under-wire with a bead head to ensure a heavier than water fly. Other anglers who really want it to sink quickly, may pinch a weighted bead, called a split shot, onto their leader several inches to a foot above the fly.

As with most streamers, you must create some action in the fly to provoke a strike. In moving water, this isn't a problem at all because the water flow itself will impart a swirl about the **Woolly Bugger's** tail to make it appear as if it were naturally swimming. When fishing in flat water like a pond or lake, the angler can create the same illusion by merely making short 2 to 8-inch strips in the fly line. The short pause between strips allows the fly to sink a bit and that action also contributes to provocative tail

undulations as if the fly is swimming downward to escape
an oncoming predator.

12—Mickey Finn

Originally named the **Red and Yellow Bucktail**,
this streamer's design is attributed to Charles Langevin
from Quebec, Canada, in the 19th century. The fly was
later renamed **The Assassin** by Gregory Clark. John
Alden Knight, an outdoor writer from Williamsport,
Pennsylvania, was responsible for popularizing a
renaming of the fly to **Mickey Finn** to memorialize the
untimely death of Rudolph Valentino to a surreptitious
overdose of barbiturates, commonly known at the time as
a "Mickey Finn".

Foster Ainsworth, in his book *The Mysteries of Trout
Fishing,* admonishes anglers to never leave home without
them. Originally developed to catch eastern brook trout,
this fly will catch numerous other species as well. For
example, west coast anglers use it for steelhead and
salmon. Warm water anglers will catch black bass and
panfish while marine fly fishers will find success using
their **Mickey Finns** for coastal predators. Obviously,
smaller sizes (8-10) are used for trout and panfish, and
larger hooks (size 2-4) are used for black bass, salmon and
coastal predators. It seems that many fish species cannot

resist the urge to eat something that is predominantly made out of dyed red and yellow bucktail hair.

13—Muddler Minnow

The **Muddler Minnow** is a great fly that has endured the test of time. It originated in the mid 1930s by angler and fly tier Don Gapen to imitate a sculpin — a small prey fish species — in the Nipigon River, Ontario, Canada.

Some anglers feature this fly among their most favorite. When fished underwater as a weighted fly, it not only suggests the common sculpin but it also has been related to minnows, crawfish, shrimp and, in smaller sizes, aquatic nymphs. Yet when fished on the surface, it resembles a larger insect like a grasshopper. To top it all off, the pattern in larger sizes can be as successful in saltwater as well as in freshwater lakes, ponds and rivers.

As noted above, it can be fished in multiple sizes. However, if I had to recommend just one size, I would pick size 8 for most freshwater applications. Nevertheless, if you are going to fish a **Muddler** in saltwater, you would want a larger size (size 2 or bigger), weighted and tied on a corrosion-resistant hook.

As with most streamers, you impart movement to the fly by stripping the fly line in flat or slow moving water.

In flowing water, you might cast it over and across in the traditional way and then allow it to dead drift with the current downstream so as not to create drag. As the fly line reaches the end of the drift, the fly will pick up speed and cross the river back to your side. If the pattern is weighted, you might even try stripping it back slowly toward you, imitating a small fish swimming back upstream, as another way of increasing a hookup.

14—Clouser Minnow

Often just called a **Clouser**, this fantastic fly was developed by Pennsylvanian Bob Clouser in the late 1980s for fishing smallmouth bass in the Susquehanna River. In his book, *Fly Fishing for Smallmouth,* Clouser introduces a retrieval technique, the Susquehanna Strip, which seems to provoke strikes as the fly moves, pauses, and then moves again. Essentially, the angler strips in about 3 feet of fly line, then pauses allowing the fly to drop toward the bottom. What makes this retrieval technique unique is the variable stripping speed. The first 2 feet are stripped more slowly followed by a much quicker strip in the last foot. Clouser advises that the strike is most likely to occur at the pause just as the fly is about to drop — so be ready to set the hook. If you don't get a strike, try repeating the stripping process once again.

The **Clouser,** my favorite is a fly tied with chartreuse and white buck tail hair is just as effective on striped bass, bluefish and other coastal predators. I have even caught tautog (black fish) and mullet on this pattern. On darker days or at night, a **Clouser** in black can be useful if you happen to have one in your fly box.

15 —⌒Deceiver

Without question, this fly is one of the great all time streamers. Developed by legendary Lefty Kreh in the late 1950s, it is one of my favorite flies. If the species you want to catch swims and eats fish, the **Deceiver** is your "go-to" fly. Lefty designed his original **Deceivers** to imitate a diversity of baitfish. He wanted a fly that could be tied in multiple lengths (from 2 to 3 inches to as much as 8 to 10 inches) where the hackle wouldn't foul around the hook bend during the cast or retrieve. He also wanted it to have minimal air resistance during casting and would present a fish-like silhouette and swimming action when underwater.   No simple task!

The **Deceiver** was initially tied in white to catch Chesapeake Bay stripped bass, and catch bass it did. In time, Lefty and others added different color collars and experimented with multiple color combinations to emulate such prey as bay anchovies, young herring or shad, menhaden, silversides, sand lances, squid and mullet. Anglers throughout the world have used this fly to catch just about every kind of marine recreational species. Freshwater anglers have caught black bass, trout and salmon, walleye and even northern pike. For most coastal predators, my personal favorite is a 3 or 4-inch fly, size 2/0, in a chartreuse and white combination.

16—Crazy Charlie

The **Crazy Charlie** was designed by Bob Nauheim in the late 1970s. As he developed his pattern, he worked with long-time Bahamian guide from Andros Island, "Bonefish" Charlie Smith. Smith provided critical insight on the behavior and preferences of bonefish. Originally intended to mimic a glass minnow, Nauheim quickly learned it was more effective fished as a shrimp. Orvis' Leigh Perkins, learned of the fly, fished them with considerable success and coined them "Crazy Charlie".

The fly generally is fished with short 1 or 2-foot strips, making it appear to skitter along the bottom creating small puffs of sand and coral grit as it hits the bottom. A bonefish recognizes this behavior as what might naturally occur when a small shrimp or crab seeks shelter in the bottom sediment. Bonefish love small shrimp and crabs so they respond very well to this prey avoidance behavior.

I am reminded by something Forrest Gump conveyed concerning the versatile and tasty shrimp and the numerous ways it can be prepared. It seems that there isn't a bad shrimp recipe. Similarly, most fish predators will not pass up an opportunity to eat a shrimp so do not restrict your use of this fly to bonefish alone. For example, several years back, I was fishing this fly in the Gulf of Mexico for sea trout and then I flew to Vancouver, British Columbia, where I used the same fly for salmon a few days later.

17 — Hornberg

Frank Hornberg was a conservation officer from Portage County, Wisconsin from 1920 until 1950. He also loved to fly fish for trout and created this classic American fly in the 1920s. The **Hornberg** fly has a provocative size and profile, great action and color and, if you need anything more, it can be equally effective fished submerged as a wet fly or on the surface as a dry.

While game warden Hornberg likely designed his fly to imitate a minnow (sizes 6 or 8), in a smaller size 14, it might easily be taken for a caddis imitation. Although I find that brook trout particularly like it fished wet, anglers have used it successfully on other species of trout and even Atlantic salmon.

I also like to fish this fly submerged as the front

attractor in tandem with a **Woolly Bugger** trailing about 18 to 20 inches behind. I believe that the **Hornberg** catches their eye and, with the **Bugger** simulating pursuit, the fish attacks the slightly larger trailer. When this deadly combination is working, fish almost always slam the trailer fly.

FIVE GREAT ATTRACTOR FLIES

Prince Nymph, Stimulator, Royal Wulff, Humpy & Bob's Banger

Attractor flies do not necessarily represent anything that naturally exists in the waters when and where you are fishing. While they may look like something to eat, their shared characteristic is that they were designed to arouse the curiosity of the fish you are seeking to catch. In general, use large and noisy flies if you don't know where the fish might be and smaller less evasive presentations when you know a fish's location. Let's look at a few of these **attractors**.

18 ⌒Royal Wulff

Hairwing flies were first promoted prior to 1890 by A.S. Trude, an angler and rancher from Idaho. From the west, the idea moved eastward to fly tiers eager to experiment with new materials and techniques.

Over the years, dry flies continue to evolve and according to one story, Reuben Cross around the late 1920s tied a hair-wing coachman at the request of his Catskill and Beaverkill Trout Club friend L.Q. Quackenbush. The fly was called **Quack's Coachman**. The fly, a variant of the popular **Royal Coachman**, substituted impala tail hair for feathers when making the wing. This modification made the fly more durable, higher floating, more aerodynamic and easier to restore to floatability after it has been wetted and slimed when a fish was caught.

Meanwhile, Lee Wulff was seeking to develop an improved dry fly to imitate better several species of mayfly from the Ausable River, NY. His first successful fly using bucktail for the wings was the **Gray Wulff**. Later variants included the **White Wulff** and, of course, the **Royal Wulff**. Lee's hairwing Wulff fly series became so popular that even though the **Quack's Coachman** might have been first, the name **Royal Wulff** is what stuck.

The **Royal Wulff** is a beautiful and highly visible fly

and is useful on darker overcast days. Also, since it sits high above the water and when viewed from below the surface, it has a bottom silhouette that seems to beg the fish to eat it. I would fish a size 14 for slow-moving or flat water while a slight larger size 12 might be a better selection for faster more turbulent streams. Lee Wulff was said to have caught Atlantic salmon on even larger size 4 **Royal Wulffs**.

19—Stimulator

Randall Kaufmann of Tigard, Oregon, wanted a new stonefly imitation to be used on higher gradient streams typical of those found in the west. His **Stimulator** floats high on the water's surface and with a low wing profile it creates an illusion of bulk. Superior buoyancy allows it to be visible by both the angler and the fish, especially in fast-moving water. Some anglers also use this buoyant fly as a strike indicator when trailing a second fly, called a dropper, tied to the **Stimulator's** hook bend.

Today, it comes in numerous color combinations (orange, yellow, olive, green, tan and black) and sizes. For example, sizes 12 and 14 in yellow imitate nicely the little stonefly; sizes 10 and 12 in green or tan emulate grasshoppers; and smaller sizes 14-16 are excellent representations of caddis flies. Don't restrict your use of this fly just to trout. In spring, I have caught lots of smallmouth bass on a bright orange **Stimulator**. When fish don't seem to be cooperating, tie on this effective attractor fly and see if you can use it to provoke a strike. Try skittering it over the water's surface in caddis-like fashion, or make it twitch as a grasshopper.

20 ⟶ Humpy

The development of this fly (also called the **Goofus Bug**) was almost certainly in the Western United States with most votes coming from around Jackson, Wyoming. Invented out of necessity for the steeper gradient streams where the water flows fast, a large, high-floating and visible fly was needed; and the **Humpy** was born.

Whatever its actual lineage, the **Humpy** satisfies all of the above needs and as a result it is extremely popular, particularly in the west. Some anglers love it so much that they fish it almost exclusively.

Although I think of it as an **attractor fly**, some anglers believe that it suggests beetles, mayflies, caddis, stoneflies or perhaps even a hellgrammite. This is a tall order for any fly but who can argue because **Humpies** do catch fish.

A **Humpy's** universal appeal comes from its high floatation profile as it rests on the water's surface. The abdomen, or rear part of the fly, can be made from red, yellow or green floss. I especially like those tied with natural green or bronze iridescent peacock hurl.

In any case, if you want to catch trout, grayling and panfish, size 14 **Humpies** will work great. Moreover, size 10 or 12 **Humpies,** being a bit larger, are excellent for largemouth and smallmouth bass.

21 —⌒Prince Nymph

Although there may be some dispute as to who originated this fly, one story holds that Dick and Don Olson of Bemidji, Minnesota, first developed the pattern. However, Californian Doug Prince, who used ostrich herl in his original body design, is given the name credit.

With life like wings on its back, this popular fly covers a broad range of aquatic nymphs. It is said that the fly's attraction results from the iridescence of the peacock herl body combined with the reflectance of the gold rib. The fly also is called the **Brown Fork Tail** because of its distinctive tail of goose biots (stiff plastic-like fibers from the leading edge of a goose's large wing feather).

When other nymphs fail to catch fish, tie on a size 14 **Prince Nymph** and dead drift it through likely fish holding areas and see if a fish takes it. I like it tied with a small black tungsten bead which gives it some weight to make it sink quickly. By using a strip, pause and strip motion, the fly will rise, dip and rise. If that doesn't provoke a fish, I don't know what will!

22—Bob's Banger

A popper, **Bob's Banger** was developed by New Jersey fly tier and angler Bob Popovics to simulate a wounded baitfish. This fly has a unique quality; its head can be pulled off while fishing and replaced by another head with a different color to give added flexibility.

A popper works by capturing a bit of air at the front of the fly. To create this action, the angler sharply **strips** the fly line. An audible pop results when the temporarily compressed air is released at the end of the strip. Black bass, walleye and coastal predators are attracted to the pop and then see the fly acting erratically swimming near the surface. To a predator, this signals an easy meal!

Fly fishing with poppers is as exciting as it gets. Not only do you get the physical tug of your line indicating a fish attached to the hook, like dry fly fishing you also get to see the drama unfold up close and personal right there on the surface. The fish smacks your fly hard and you see it happen. Wow, that is fun!

Bob's Banger is a simple yet durable fly — one

that can withstand the violent assault imposed by a large, powerful and often toothy predator. Like many saltwater flies, I recommend one predominantly dressed in chartreuse and white. Size 1/0 is a good place to start. It fishes well early in the morning when the water is calm and again later in the afternoon or early evening. Vary the stripping speed until you find one that is comfortable for you and, most importantly, catches fish. Of course, if you really want a blast, feel free to cast it into a school of feeding predators any time of the day. Hold on!

TWO GREAT EMERGER FLIES

23—CDC emerger

In my earlier book, *Learn to Fly Fish in 24 Hours*, I featured and showed how to tie the **CDC emerger**. I am not its originator and unfortunately I just can't remember who taught it to me. Nevertheless, perhaps Gary LaFontaine's **Emergent Sparkle Pupa** (size 16) served as the inspiration. Orvis and Dan Bailey's (www.dan-bailey.com) offers the best commercially available imitations I can find. Orvis lists it as the **Hare Emerger** (J93PG). Bailey's call it the **CDC Sparkle Dun** in dark and light olive, sizes 18 and 20.

So when you see trout sipping something small off the surface and need a very small fly to match a tiny caddis or mayfly as it emerges from its **nymphal shuck**, dig into your fly box for the **CDC Emerger.** At the same time, be sure to reduce the size of your tippet to a 6X or smaller so as not to influence unnaturally the fly's drift downstream.

This fly is effective in slow clear water on the dead drift. Also, I catch a lot of fish when I allow the fly to submerge at the end of the drift. As the fly moves back across to my side of the river, the CDC feathers become wet and flutter in the current. I believe that the flutter is more than most trout can handle and the chase is on! Since the fly line is already taught, hook setting is generally easier. Also, I like to strip the fly back upstream toward me, and the jerky swimming motion I create by making short strips is likely to provoke strikes as well.

24—The Usual

This design is generally attributed to Francis Betters of New York. As the story goes, one of his angling pals, Bill Phillips, liked the pattern so well that he used it all the time. When friends asked which fly he used, his reply was "**The Usual**." The fly's name was thus coined and it stuck. So, what exactly is **The Usual**?

The Usual is a durable fly that uses the foot hair of the snowshoe hare as a tail, body and wing. It is tied with red thread giving it a fish-attractive red head. Betters acknowledges it to be a representation of nothing in particular. Some anglers believe it to suggest a Hendrickson mayfly but what the fish speculate it to be is anyone's guess.

I like to fish it wet, size 14, as an emerger. However, dressed with dry fly floatant and with air trapped between its component hair fibers, it floats well and is easily fished as a dry fly. If you don't tie flies yet, you may have to go a little out of your way to purchase them. Contact Rodney at Flagg's Fly and Tackle (978-544-0034) in Orange, Massachusetts, tell him you want "**The Usual**" and he will get them out to you right away. One on-line source is the Adirondack Sport Shop, www.ausablewulff.com.

SUMMARY

There your have them — a great selection of 24 time and field-tested flies that work! You don't have to go off and fill your fly boxes with the many thousands of patterns offered by this or that angler or fly shop. I certainly am not saying that you can't add from time to time another fly to your favorite patterns. What I am saying, however, is that using the flies described above will catch most fish predators anywhere in the world most of the time.

While we are still on flies, let me review a few more critical principles of fly fishing. Over the years of fishing and teaching people to fly fish, the one consistent thing I've learned is that no matter the type of fly — wet or dry, the pattern or the size of the hook, the angler must maintain good line control. This means that in order to set the hook should a fish strike your fly, there cannot be excessive slack in the fly line. Stating this important point another way, if there is too much loose line between the fly and the hand you use to set the hook, the fish will have a huge advantage by spitting the hook before it becomes impaled in its mouth. A fish, especially a selective feeder, will often take a fly into its mouth believing it is something to eat. However, if the texture is not familiar, it may almost instantaneously reject it. Real bugs, small fish and most other edible natural prey, may crunch, tear or break into smaller pieces when bitten. They may also flow unrestricted into the fish's mouth. Artificial flies, with leaders attached are designed to appear real but — are not! A fish expects your fly to behave in a certain way and when it doesn't, it often will be rejected in an instant.

In order for you to catch, that is, hook that fish, you may have less than a second to set the hook, a term used to describe imbedding the hook into the fish's cartilaginous mouth. If there is too much slack in your fly line, there is a great risk that the fish will take your fly, assess its texture, feel its not free floating and spit it before you can possibly strip back the fly line sufficiently tight enough to cause the hook's point to penetrate a fish's mouth parts, especially those with particularly hard boney-like jaws.

For example, if you are fishing and casting your way upstream, fly line slack has to be removed as the fly drifts downstream toward you. I remember one time particularly when I made what I thought was a beautiful presentation upstream. I just enjoyed the cast and, unfortunately for me, forgot to take up the fly line slack. When the fish slammed my fly, I was startled. When it spit the hook, I called myself a few choice names.

There are several ways to address this problem and all require attention by the angler. After the fly comes to rest on the water, you must begin to strip back the fly line continuously at the same rate of your fly's downstream drift. For example, if the downstream drift is two feet per second, your strip rate should also approximate two feet per second.

Another successful technique to remove the slack is to progressively raise your rod tip as your fly continues its downstream drift and passes you. Effective particularly on slower drifts, this line control method has another big advantage and that is it can let you add fly line to extend the drag free drift downstream. Here, you merely lower your rod tip in the downstream direction thereby returning to the water the fly line you drew off earlier. At the end of the drift, you can even extend your rod and rod hand toward the fly to get a few extra inches of drag free drift.

A smallmouth bass rises for a fly.

When fishing a dry fly, the fly at the end of the drift will begin to "feel" the drag of the fly line and pick up speed. It will begin to skitter across the surface until it reaches a point directly downstream of your rod tip. There may be so much tension on the fly at this moment that it will be drawn underwater. Here you have two choices: 1) fish it back upstream underwater as a wet fly or 2) immediately go into a casting sequence and bring the fly back upstream for yet another drift. Obviously, both techniques can catch fish so from time to time use both and see what happens.

When fishing a wet fly, especially a nymph, the downstream current at the end of the drift will begin to drag the fly line as well. Your fly, being underwater at some depth, will increase speed. However, there is a major difference in that the fly also will begin to lift toward the surface. Fish have seen natural emerging insects race toward the surface before and recognize this as a familiar prey behavior. Often the impulse is to strike and strike quickly before the rising bug reaches the water/air interface and flies away. Many times, an angler will be rewarded with a catch as the fly lifts from the bottom. Note the fly line is already taught, the fly has momentum and the fish is actively pursuing it. Since effective line control is established, the fish will often hook itself and the angler gets credit for the catch. Not too shabby!

FOUR

BALANCED FLY TACKLE

To begin our adventure, we must first assemble the fly fishing equipment you will use. My hope is that you will develop an almost emotional bond with your favorite gear not so unlike how Eric Clapton feels about his vintage Fender Stratocaster guitar. To achieve that goal, the equipment must be comfortable, reliable and time-tested. It needs to do exactly as you wish. Only a balanced outfit will do it all.

In this chapter we will discuss the size of the rig as it pertains to the relative size of the fish being sought. It is just not much fun catching very small fish on a heavy weight rod. As hard as it might try, the fish would not make any significant bend in the rod and the angler would merely reel it in — no challenge there!

Conversely, most fair-minded anglers understand that using a light weight rod for very large fish is nonsense. Even if we were lucky enough to hook successfully such a trophy, the equipment would likely be destroyed by the shear power of the fish. More importantly, fishery scientists and responsible anglers would agree that ultimately landing a very large fish on overly lightweight equipment is absurdly unfair to the fish. Should this fish be released after the battle even if it appears to happily swim away, acid accumulation in its muscles might make it difficult if not impossible to survive yet another 24 hours.

Fly rods vary in size and are commonly available from 1-weight all the way up to 15-weight. Higher number rods have greater spine strength and can successfully battle increasingly larger fish. While there may be some exceptions, generally rods rated 8-weight or higher are used for salmon, dorado or fishing for larger saltwater species. At the other end of the spectrum, lower rated rods are normally reserved for smaller freshwater fish.

Different size fly rods are used to match more closely the size fish expected to be caught. The heavier weight rod at the top of the photo has a fighting butt to give extra leverage for trying to land that big one.

The goal here is to help you determine the size of equipment that best suits the size of fish that you are most likely to catch. Fly rod manufacturers try to follow industry standards where a given rod weight designation will efficiently cast a line of the same weight designation. Indeed, the industry has become so good at designing fly rods that almost any decent rod today can easily be loaded with fly line a weight above or below the specified rod weight. For example, a 5-weight rod, a favorite of many freshwater anglers, can be fished with a 5-weight line, a 4-weight line and even a 6-weight line. Similarly, an 8-weight rod, a common saltwater rig, can use 7 to 9-weight fly lines.

ROD WEIGHT AND EXPECTED FISH SIZE

The purpose of matching the rod size with the fish you are trying to catch is to give you and the fish a sporting chance. As a responsible angler, you want to give the fish a reasonable expectation that it will survive should you desire to release it. If you overmatch the rod with the fish, you won't have as much fun. Conversely, if you catch a larger fish on a lighter rod, you may not be able to land the fish or more likely tire it beyond recovery. The below table provides a guide to rod selection.

Rod Weight	Fish Size
1-3	1 pound or less
4-5	1 - 3 pounds
6-7	3 - 5 pounds
8-9	5 - 20 pounds
10-12	Larger than 20 lbs

I recommend beginning anglers increase or up weight their fly line by one weight over the rod designation. In so doing, the extra weight of the fly line as it moves through the air during the casting motion gives added cues to the caster when the rod is loaded fully during the backcast. This enhanced feel helps the angler better understand the critical timing necessary to begin an effective delivery of the fly during the forward cast.

Desired Rod Tip Path

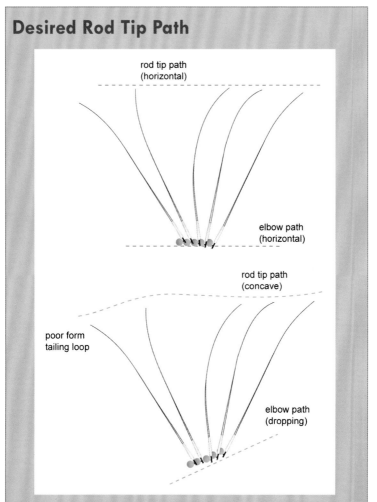

rod tip path
(horizontal)

elbow path
(horizontal)

rod tip path
(concave)

poor form
tailing loop

elbow path
(dropping)

Overweighting the fly line too much may increase stress on the rod's shaft and cause it to bend too much or even break. Moreover, the increased bend initiated by the weight of the fly line going backward and increased as thumb pressure is exerted in the forward casting motion will cause the rod tip to dip below the desired straight line path. A tailing loop will develop and a "wind knot" is sure to follow. Keep your elbow path horizontal.

Casting with balanced tackle will also reduce fatigue. If you fish all day as I sometimes do, you may make hundreds if not thousands of casts. If your equipment is way out of balance, your arm will become tired and you will not enjoy the experience as you might otherwise.

Fly reels need to be matched to their proposed use. Big fish may require smooth and effective drag systems and large arbor reels that have a greater capacity to hold more backing.

Let's assume that you have a matched (equal to or plus or minus one weight) fly line mounted on a reel proportioned to the rod. One way to help reduce casting fatigue is to see where the balance of the rod actually is located. To do this, draw from the reel about 30 feet of fly line or the amount of line you will most likely be casting. This length should extend beyond the rod tip. Now with your index finger supporting the cork handle, move the finger to where the rod balances. At this point and keeping your index finger at the balance point, grip your hand to the handle with your thumb on top of the rod. A properly balanced rod will naturally position your thumb between a half-inch and an inch away from the top of the cork grip. This position is important because the backcast is powered by your fingers while the forward cast is powered by your thumb. If half the rod weight is above the index finger and half below it, the casting motion flows smoothly between the two and your arm won't be so fatigued after a day of fishing.

Finding the balance point of a fly rod is critical for hand placement and fatigue reduction. Note the forefinger placement. To approximate an actual fishing situation, draw off the reel 30' of fly line before determining your rod's balance point.

With the balance point found, simply fold the remaining fingers around the cork handle griping the rod.

Now that you have the rod and line balanced, we will move on to the leader. There is a rule of thumb that you can use to help balance the leader to the fly. To determine the correct leader/tippet size, simply divide the hook size you intend to use by 3. For example, if you intend to use a size 12 fly, a size 4X tippet will do just fine. As you might expect, this is just a guide, so you might be able to get away with size 3X or 5X tippet sizes as well. Nevertheless, tangles and line twists may result if you use finer tippet (sizes 6X, 7X or 8X) with size 12 or larger flies.

Conversely, tippet sizes larger than 3X may make your fly drift unnaturally or the heavier leader (2X or larger) may be so awkward that it might be seen by the fish. To repeat, your goal is to use a tippet that matches the fly fine enough that you don't get line twist yet not so large that it makes your fly appear to be unnatural in or on the water.

TIPPET

The end section of a tapered leader is often called the tippet. Selecting the appropriate tippet size can assist in making a better presentation of the fly and also minimizes line twists and tangles caused by using a big fly with a light tippet. To estimate proper tippet size, divide the hook size of the fly you wish to use by 3 (Rule of Three). For example, if you want to use a size 12 fly, use a 4X tippet (12/3=4). While there might be some variability between tippet manufacturers, the table below should serve as a fairly good guide.

Tippet Size	Pound Test	Fly Sizes
03X	22	3/0 - 5/0
02X	19	1/0-2/0
01X	16	4 – 1/0
0X	14	6 - 2
1X	12	8 - 4
2X	10	10 - 6
3X	8	12 - 8
4X	6	14 - 10
5X	4	18 - 12
6X	3	20 - 16
7X	2	24 - 20
8X	1	28 - 24

Lastly, let's talk about keeping balance, particularly when standing on slippery rocks with sloshing water all about you. It is really difficult to concentrate on catching fish when you are worried that your feet may slip out from beneath you at any moment. Here you may be wishing that you were wearing proper footwear. Please consider getting comfortable and secure boots or wading shoes. Pay special attention to the soles. Felt soles are great for most wading situations but when it gets ultra slick, studded soles may be more appropriate. Local information obtained at a nearby fly shop might provide you some valued advice on what sole is best for the area you plan to fish. One company (Korkers) offers a shoe with an exchangeable bottom. Aside from the obvious traction advantages, a quick removal of your studded soles before getting into a rubber-bottomed raft will make your guide happier!

Some wading boot manufacturers use interchangeable soles to give anglers choice for maintaining balance when wading about slippery river bottoms.

Another aid you may wish to use is a wading staff. I call this my third leg and when I find myself in water a bit deeper or swifter than I expected, I whip out my foldable wading staff and jam it into the bottom. The one I really like is a Folstaf as it is reliable and sturdy. It uses an internal bungee cord and interlocking aluminum sections. Once released from its holster, it takes a second to spring together and be ready to help you stabilize your footing.

In summary, casting a balanced rig is good for the equipment; everything works together. Most importantly, it is good for you as you won't get fatigued from making repetitive casts. Clearly, this is poetry in motion.

CHAPTER

FIVE

How to Deliver Your Fly to a Spot

Now that you have the balanced equipment assembled and ready to go, we need to discuss how to deliver the fly to a specific spot — hopefully one that holds a fish! While it may be an understatement it nevertheless holds true: if a fish sees your fly, you will have a much better chance at catching it. Learning how to deliver your fly to a determined location in front of a fish is a skill you will need to learn. Only practice and experience will bring you to a level of competency to present your fly efficiently each and every time. This should be your goal.

I focus on casting because it is the only way to get the fly to the fish. If I were standing next to you, I could tie on the precise fly that the fish are hammering. I might even suggest to you where you might want to drop your fly. In the end, however, it really is up to you to make the cast, aim and have the fly drop into the fish's feeding window without alerting the fish to your presence. If you do it correctly, your fly has a great chance of appearing as if it were a natural prey and something the fish cares to eat. Miss that spot and the fish may never even see the fly. If it can't see your fly, the fish is most unlikely to make an "eat" decision and the fly get walloped.

There are two basic casting techniques: the roll cast

How to make a Roll Cast

⎯◦ Grasp the rod handle comfortably with your thumb positioned on top.

⎯◦ Raise the rod tip slowly to the one o'clock position.

⎯◦ Have the rod lean out and away from you. The reel front should be pointing toward the water.

⎯◦ Take a breath.

⎯◦ Initiate the cast by exerting firm forward pressure with your thumb. The motion is not so unlike trying to hit a nail with a hammer. Like with a hammer, your wrist and forearm should increasingly accelerate being pushed forward with firm thumb pressure.

⎯◦ When the rod tip reaches the 10 o'clock position, pause or slow the forward progression of the rod allowing the fly line above you to unroll and straighten to flow out toward your target. The line will always go in the direction you point the rod tip.

and the traditional backcast. Both need to be learned and practiced. The traditional backcast is the one most often seen on TV or in the movies where the angler lifts the line from the water and propels it rearward. The angler stops the fly rod at the one o'clock position and waits until the line fully unfurls rearward. When the line is straight out behind and before the line sags and begins to fall, the angler exerts forward thumb pressure pushing the rod forward, pauses the rod tip slightly at the 10 o'clock position until the forward loop takes shape, and delivers the fly in the direction dictated by the rod tip.

I like to think of the roll cast as half a traditional cast. It is simple to learn and is so effective. So while most fly fishing schools and publications emphasize and spend most of their time on the traditional backcast, I will focus on a casting technique that you must master to become a competent angler. I am not saying that the traditional backcast is not imperative for you to learn. It most certainly is. Rather, I want you to take a bit more time to understand how useful the simple roll cast can be.

Master the roll cast

When we were younger and our knees more solid, my wife and I did a bit of downhill skiing. While I progressed along and could parallel ski, she never went beyond the snowplow. Wherever we went from the bunny slope to the mogul fields, she would snowplow — and snowplow she could. Using that one basic skiing technique she could safely descend any slope. She was having fun!

A similar example exists in fly fishing and, more specifically, fly casting. The easiest cast to learn, and arguably the most successful at catching fish, is the roll cast.

The one thing I would emphasize to an aspiring angler is to learn the roll cast thoroughly. It is the simplest of all casting motions yet can present your fly delicately and effectively. Two handed Spey casting using 15-foot fly rods, a style of fly delivery more common to Europe, is merely a roll cast modification.

I know that everyone wants to perfect the beautiful traditional backcast symbolic of the sport quickly. Similarly, these folks also want to cast long distances — perhaps to the other side of the river where the fishing is *always* better. In fact, more fish are caught by the best anglers within 30 feet of where they are standing. The roll cast can very easily deliver your fly to these distances. Perfect the roll cast and you will be rewarded with successful catches. In this section I will briefly describe how to make an effective roll cast and then explore what an effective roll cast can do for you.

Remember, the first 30 feet of a weight forward (WF) fly line has most of the weight needed to present your fly. When you first arrive at your fishing location, you will need to get some line out onto the water so that you can begin to fish. In all likelihood the terminal end of the fly line will be positioned near the end of the fly rod near the **tip top** (line guide at the end of the fly rod). Now strip or draw out past the tip top about 5 to 7 yards of fly line from the reel. This is all you need to get started.

Begin a roll cast by bringing your fly rod tip to the one o'clock position with the rod at a slight angle leaning away from you and have the front of the reel facing the water. Relax. To begin the cast, move your hand and forearm forward with increasing speed, exert forward thumb pressure until the rod tip reaches the 10 o'clock position where you will pause or at least slow the forward motion of the rod. The momentary pause at 10 o'clock allows the tip of the fly rod to stabilize while the fly line straightens out above you and begins flowing in the direction of your target. The roll cast is completed as you follow through by gradually lowering the rod tip to a position parallel to the water. Remember, a bit of practice will get the motion and timing down and before you know it, you will become a competent roll caster.

I mentioned that the first thing a roll cast can do for you is to get some line out onto the water. From there you can draw more line from the reel to extend your casting distance. This is done by slowly raising your rod tip to the one o'clock position. With additional line off the reel and lying loosely at your feet (be careful not to step on it), hold the fly line between the reel and the first stripping guide with your non-casting hand. Grasp the line firmly through the roll cast and release it precisely as you pause the rod at the 10 o'clock position during the forward stroke. The timing of the release is critical and must occur as your fly line begins to stream forward. With a bit of practice, you will learn how to shoot fly line in a roll cast in a way to present your fly to a distant target exceeding 30 feet.

(a)   (b)

In (a), raise the rod tip and stop it at the 1 o'clock position. Relax. Check that the reel is pointed in the direction
you want to cast and that the rod is slightly leaning
away from you. Then in (b), after applying firm thumb
pressure in the forward direction, the rod tip is paused at
the 10 o'clock position to allow the loop to form and the fly
line unfurl in the direction indicated by your rod tip.

Perhaps the best application for a roll cast is when you have a wall of brush, a tree or rock ledges behind you precluding the use of a traditional backcast. Here the only option you may have is a roll cast. Don't fret — many anglers catch lots of fish using this most basic casting technique. Further, there are days when I'm fishing under the hemlocks or other dense vegetation, and the only cast I can make is the roll cast. By holding the rod to the side, you will learn to deliver a fly under an overhanging tree or, when lowering the rod across your body, back upstream upon completion of your fly reaching the end of its downstream drift.

Another important use of the roll cast is to get some fly line straightened out in front of you. From this position you can go into a **traditional backcast** and then **shoot** additional lengths of fly line during the forward casting stroke. When you get the feel of the roll cast, you might even apply a **water haul** to help load your fly rod as you begin to draw the fly rod rearward. The extra drag of the fly line and fly on the water as you draw the tip of your fly rod rearward will impart additional energy to the fly rod during the backcast stroke. This added energy will translate to faster line speed, and the faster the line moves the farther it will travel during the forward casting stroke.

A somewhat unconventional use of a roll cast is to free your fly when it is caught on some object. For example, if you are fishing upstream and your fly becomes impaled on the upstream side of a log or rock. If you have to wade upstream to free it by hand, you most likely will put any fish in the area into an alert mode. Often, however, a quick roll cast further upstream beyond the entrapped fly will dislodge it permitting you to continue fishing.

Remember, in a roll cast or a traditional backcast the fly always goes in the direction you point the rod tip. Understanding this point is critical to placing your fly in the direction you want it to go. Of course, the second element of an accurate cast is judging the distance to the target.

While your casting hand provides the energy and direction of the cast, it is your non-casting hand that best regulates the casting distance. Your non-casting hand, by releasing at the appropriate moment, can contribute additional fly line to the forward cast. With practice, this hand can help the line feed freely for longer casts or braking the line's forward progress by intentionally pinching it at the appropriate moment as the fly appears to be reaching its target.

The left pinching hand, held off to the side, makes an "O" to allow the fly line to shoot smoothly forward during the cast.

A right hander can pinch the fly line in the left hand and hold it slightly off to the side as the casting sequence begins.

Judging distance is a skill that will develop the more you cast. Like a golfer who practices on a putting green to refine his/her touch, a fly angler should continue to polish casting skills. Even when water is not available, quickly setting up and casting to a paper plate target range on a nearby lawn is often better than watching some uninteresting show on TV. At the least, you have a fly rod in hand and can dream about your next fly fishing adventure!

CHAPTER

SIX

WHERE ARE THE FISH?

(FISH HABITAT)

I n order to catch fish consistently, you have to know where to find them. Perhaps this goes without saying: you won't catch many fish if you consistently fish in places where there are no fish! To become an effective angler, you must understand the second part of the *'where are the fish puzzle'*; namely, what brings fish to these preferred habitats? So first, to bring everyone to the same page, let's start with an overview of what is a habitat.

Everyone lives where they do for a reason — mostly because they are able to make a living and derive some degree of happiness and satisfaction as they go about their daily business. No matter where you travel, each location is special with no two places being exactly alike. To anyone who would ask, I offer this advice: *when you go to a new place especially in a foreign land, find out what makes this area unique. It may take a bit of effort on your part but the reward may very well become a lifetime experience. When you do discover that special quality, I encourage you to immerse yourself into it and enjoy the adventure to its fullest.*

In an aquatic parallel, fish live where they do because that location fulfills a matrix of necessities needed to sustain it over daily, seasonal or annual periods. In other words, the fish is taking advantage of every aspect of its local aquatic environment. When conditions change and a critical need is no longer met, the fish must move on. Such movements may be a matter of just a few feet or of many, many miles.

In the natural world, conditions are always changing. Each day modifies one factor or another so nothing is quite as stable as it might sometimes appear. Fish species have evolved to adapt to this dynamic array of change. A fish lives to see another day as a direct result of its amazing ability to adjust — a trait that goes to its very primordial core. This ability makes a fish be what it is and why it is so special; it is a member of a described species.

All of the above serves to lead into our understanding of habitat. A fish's habitat is a unique combination of the physical attributes of a given area and the environmental conditions that prevail at that moment. For example, a stream or lake bottom may have rocks, gravel, mud or sand. Add in the effects of water temperature, wind, tide, wave action, sunlight, downstream water flow, imbedded gasses including carbon dioxide and oxygen, salinity, dissolved minerals, turbidity from suspended solids, and perhaps hundreds of other minor factors, and it begins to look like home.

The biological or living component is what makes it all come together. What distinguishes our world from Mars, for instance, is the numerous and profound modifications imposed by all of the ever interacting living things. These diverse plants and animals, many microscopic, dwell, eat and reproduce here and have done so for billions of years. Their simple presence multiplies the complexity of the environment by orders of magnitude. The biological impact is so vast that our world, Earth, is unique. Each day brilliant astronomers locate more and more planets outside our solar system and to date we know of no other in the entire universe where life exists — in any form!

So a fish is where it is for at least one of several reasons. Perhaps it is just moving through to get to another place or it may be involved in a reproductive ballet to ensure the species' long term survival. For the most part, these behaviors are seasonal. The act of feeding (or at least snapping at our fly) is something near and dear to all fly anglers because that is how we catch them. With the notable exception of some anadromous species like salmon that do not eat when they return to their natal river to spawn, most fish must eat to survive and they typically do so often.

A fish's habitat then is an aquatic environment that has been significantly influenced by the many biological creatures that live there. Fish go to these preferred locations to interact with the other creatures that are already there. If the attraction is fish of the same species, perhaps the reason is to fulfill a mating function. But because fish feed or are at least looking for food almost constantly, the most likely reason is that the fish came to this place to seek something to eat. If it finds a meal, perhaps it stays. If not, it might move along to somewhere else. Simply put, as an angler you will want to fish in places that fish frequent to eat.

With our new understanding, let's look as some typical aquatic habitats that most often will attract and hold fish. Some will maintain fish seasonally, while others will hold fish throughout the year. The common trait shared by each of these habitats is that they attract smaller fish and other prey and that these, in turn, attract larger fish. If you can find the prey, the predator is probably somewhere nearby. One last point is to be aware that there may be a seasonal or perhaps even daily attraction.

Fish may not always be in these habitats but because of the prevailing conditions may appear during a given season or perhaps even during a particular time of day or night.

OUTFLOWS

As water exits a stream, estuary, or spring, it may well have different qualities than the water it is entering. For example, when a freshwater coastal river enters a saltwater bay, in addition to water of a different temperature, it brings with it a fresh supply of terrestrial nutrients. Submerged aquatic vegetation and microscopic plants called phytoplankton rapidly absorb these nutrients and use them to grow and reproduce. As the population of plants increase, so to will the diverse group of smaller invertebrate animals like rotifers, scuds and insects grazing on the plants. In the cycle of life, next to benefit are the little fish that forage on the invertebrates, closely followed by ever larger fish that eat their smaller cousins. Here, where prey fish abound, I would likely use a streamer fly, particularly one that looks like a small fish.

Water flow out of a coastal estuary into a large bay. Large predators are often found lurking in these outflows.

INFLOWS

Similar to above where a stream enters a lake or bay, it is often an opportunity for a fish to forage on a continuous flow of food floating on or within the oncoming water. Be it bugs, worms, aquatic invertebrates or smaller fish, all can be washed downstream especially from an upstream storm event. Larger predators seem to know this and often will sit and wait to see what meal happens to come their way. As the faster flowing water from the stream slows when it enters the bay, lake or estuary, so too will the heavier organisms tend to fall out. To get a meal, the fish merely has to hold its position near where the flow decreases and then select each meal as it comes. Because of the downstream dietary diversity, most wet flies including streamers and nymphs will work well as you cast over and across the inflow plume. Remember also to strip the fly line back toward you in short herky-jerky (1 or 2-inch) strips prior to the next cast.

Channels of water flowing into an estuary will hold feeding predators patiently waiting for the next meal to come to them.

POOLS BELOW RIFFLES

Note that there is again a thread of similarity to the outflows and inflows above as the predator waits for the oncoming current to bring it a meal in the well-oxygenated water below a riffle. Unfortunately, however, unless it can hold below a rock, log or ledge, it will be exposed to a somewhat faster current and have to expend a bit more energy to stay in its desired feeding lane.

With a diversity of dietary items flowing downstream, fish it as you would an inflow using streamers and nymphs. If there is a hatch, try to match using one of your dry fly patterns.

On steep gradient streams, fish the pools between the riffles.

Look for pools along small streams. A dry fly placed
a few feet upstream of the log in the center of the photo
will certainly provoke a strike. Watch your line control
by taking up slack as the fly drifts toward you.

The edges of this pool will hold fish. Place your fly just
to the side of the white water and the nearside rock.
Then, try the far side along the fallen log at the top of
the photo.

UNDERWATER STRUCTURE AND DEBRIS PILES

Angler casting to a small submerged rock pile. Underwater structures such as these rocks will surely hold some predators.

When you see anything rising from a relatively uniform bottom think predator ambush site. Many predators like to expend the least amount of effort feeding. Over time they have come to learn that most structures and debris piles, natural or manmade, attract smaller fish to forage for the numerous invertebrates that cling in and among any object rising above the bottom. An alert smaller fish can, at the first sign of a predator's approach, dart back into spaces unreachable by the larger fish. Occasionally, however, one may swim unsuspectingly toward a completely still predator that merely has to quickly open its mouth to create a suction that draws the smaller fish into its waiting maw. Casting to these fish attractors can be very productive but be aware that once hooked, the predator, like the small fish mentioned above, is likely to seek protection in the interior of the structure as well. Your job is to quickly exert line tension and move your rod tip in the opposite direction and fight the fish in open water. If you win this battle, you may land the fish. If not, in addition to seeing the fish break free, you might very well end up loosing your tippet and fly.

A likely fish holding pocket is just downstream of the logs and debris pile. Probe these areas with your flies. I'd use one of my bead head nymphs initially or perhaps a dry fly if I saw signs of surface feeding.

DROP OFFS

A drop off is created where a relatively shallow bottom rapidly falls off to much deeper water. Underwater cliffs, submerged channel beds or steeply descending seamounts are all examples. Other less dramatic, yet no less effective fishing opportunities, include small ledges or rock steps as might occur in a river bed or a beach that falls away quickly just beyond the surf line. Predators commonly use a drop off because it gives them deeper water protection from being eaten themselves as well as the ideal site to see what might be happening above them. From the safety of the deep, they can launch an attack when the chances of success move in their favor. In high current situations, a drop off can offer some protection from the brunt of the water flow yet provide a great upstream observation post to see anything edible heading its way. Again, streamer flies and weighted nymphs are excellent choices to probe the margins of the drop off.

Fish along submerged weed lines and drop offs.

Try fishing the drop off where there is water movement.
Baitfish move through these areas and become easy prey.

THERMAL REFUGIA

One summer a few years back I was fishing for smallmouth bass in the lower Deerfield River in western Massachusetts. As I was wading along, I noted a small side channel backwater created as the river level receded. What attracted my attention was that the water coming out of the backwater was clear and much colder than the mainstem river water. Following the side channel upstream a few yards, I saw a pile of trout, mostly rainbows, stacked up in there partially covered by some low-hanging vegetation. With the water depth between 1 and 2 feet, the fish were very nervous. To some degree they must have been visible from the air, so I am sure the local ospreys were getting fat on them. The primary reason these fish were attracted to this side channel was because a cold spring was upwelling from the bottom and trout have a strong thermal preference for colder water.

In winter, the converse is also true. If there are warm water springs in your area, ask around to see if anyone has had fishing success. Another possibility, while not quite a product of nature but nonetheless more common, are power plant cooling plumes. Electric utility plants often discharge large quantities of heated water into lakes, bays, estuaries or their own cooling ponds. Sometimes, even in the dead of winter, a small closed ecosystem more indicative of summer can be established and sustained by warm water discharge. Predators and prey move about these warmer waters oblivious to the frigid conditions just outside their artificial world. When accessible and legal to do so (note there may well be restrictions on approaching a power plant), your fly fishing does not have to suffer despite cold air temperatures outside.

Tailwaters are a third form of refugia. These areas are named for the river (as viewed from the air it appears as if it is an animal's tail) flowing out from the base of a dam. The lake above the dam appears as if it is the animal's body. In many cases, dam operators are required as part of their license to maintain a minimal instream flow. If the released water discharge comes from water at the dam's base, it generally is colder in summer and warmer in winter. Because the water temperatures do not deviate greatly all year long, tailwaters can sustain a fish population not characteristically found in that region.

Thermal refugia for several reasons may be difficult to fish. First, the fish may be very nervous from having to worry constantly about predator attacks. Also, tailwaters and springs often get enhanced fishing pressure by avid anglers who come to these areas when it might be the only game in town. If the water is clear and slow moving, fish have a long time to look at your fly and determine if it is natural looking. Ultra small flies (size 22 to 28) on very fine tippet often rule in these circumstances.

Cooling water plumes, meanwhile, can be very productive. Predators are looking for something to eat and at certain times of the year the prey base may be quite low so large fish-like streamer flies can be excellent imitations to use. **Clousers**, **Deceivers**, **Woolly Buggers** and **Mickey Finns** should all catch fish.

POINTS

Anglers fishing from a point of land that juts out into a bay. Predators often linger near this type of structure to await the movement of unsuspecting baitfish.

Besides sticking out into a bay, lake or impoundment, a point also may offer a convenient fishing location where two different water masses come together and mix, making an ideal place to fish. Predators often patrol these areas to take advantage of any prey moving across the shallows near where the point recedes underwater. If there are large rocks near the point, predators may establish ambush positions nearby from which they can attack any unsuspecting prey coming from the opposite direction. Again, streamer flies are an excellent choice to probe these areas, especially during dusk, dawn or at night. Remember, use stealth in your approach.

ENRICHMENT AREAS

What first comes to mind are areas where nutrient rich water flowing off the land enters an estuary. While this fits the criteria for an enrichment area, it isn't exactly what I am trying to suggest. Some years ago when I was in grad school, I would stop on my way home and fish off a dock that jutted out into a tidal river. Besides the dock providing great access to the water, it allowed me to make casts toward the local sewage treatment plant outflow plume. While at first this might seem distasteful, let me assure you that modern treatment plants discharge a fairly clean product. In many cases, it has lots of nutrients and many microscopic animals that little fish just love to eat. Again, where little fish congregate, predators are usually found nearby. So when I would make my casts to the plume, I was often rewarded with a nice fish to take home for dinner.

TIDAL RIPS

As fast-moving tidal water moves from a relatively deep area onto a more shallow shelf, the water increases speed and is forced upward creating an area of aggressive turbulence. Smaller fish getting caught up in this washing machine like cauldron are very vulnerable to larger predators looking for something to eat. Use caution when fishing these areas as conditions can become quite hazardous due to large breaking waves. Don't go into a tidal rip unless you really know what you are doing. If, however, your watercraft can approach a tidal rip safely, fishing any small fish imitation pattern, especially one that is slightly weighted, often will find a predator.

Fishing into the plume of a tidal rip is often rewarded with catches of large predators waiting for vulnerable baitfish.

SHADED AREAS

Predators and prey commonly are attracted to low-hanging trees, docks, buoys, and almost anything floating about. Seaweed mats and tidal foam lines should always be probed by a cast or two. A friend also told me that he has caught fish by casting alongside a floating wooden freight pallet. Some years ago, I fished a river in the Amazon system where there was a dense floating vegetative mat extending several yards from the river bank on both sides of the channel. Drifting along in a boat propelled by the downstream current, I was casting a heavily weighted **Clouser.** I caught many peacock bass. The fish were waiting underneath the vegetation just on the edge of the open water. As soon as the fly hit the water and quickly began to sink, the predator would attack.

undercut banks and open areas below old tree roots are excellent holdings areas for wary fish. When you hook a fish you may have to use your fly rod to keep the fish from seeking the protection of roots and snags.

Floating debris lines often attract and hold predators. Cast to the edge and be ready for a quick strike.

Successful largemouth bass anglers often cast to the sides and ends of any small piers or boat docks. Bass are attracted to these overhead structures while waiting for some meal to swim their way. Don't hesitate to cast near lily pads and other surface vegetation.   Again, if you happen to hook a fish, you will have to direct it forcefully in the opposite direction so the fish does not become entangled in any underwater roots, stems or the structure itself.

UPWELLINGS

Some of the biggest and most well-known fisheries in the world are sustained when large volumes of cool nutrient rich water are lifted from the deep and brought to the surface where sunlight and phytoplankton, small microscopic aquatic plants, begin an extraordinary cycle of biological activity. Georges Bank on the northeast coast and the western shore of South America are notable examples. With plants growing actively, a grazing population of small animals expands to take advantage of the wealth. Characteristically, a population of small fish expands as well and the predators are soon to move in to eat anything they can catch. While upwellings are not commonly found close to shore, they can be excellent places to find fish willing to take your streamer fly.

SHORELINES

Many anglers frequent exposed shorelines where wave action creates an environment that attracts prey and predators. Anyone who approaches these dynamic habitats must use good judgment and a reasonable caution because one strong wave can quickly undermine your footing and carry you out to sea. Nevertheless, it is amazing how close some of these large predators will come to shore.

Occasionally, you will see these big fish only a few yards from the beach — well within casting distance. Crab, shrimp and streamer patterns will often provoke a strike.

Casting just beyond the surf line can bring strikes from predators that move along beaches in scoured trenches created by pounding waves.

As the sun is setting, predators may venture closer to the shore to feed on unsuspecting prey. Move slowly and quietly and watch for signs of prowling fish.

SHOALS

Shoals can be great places to look for fish, especially during the spring when larger fish like smallmouth bass use them for nesting. Look for the lighter colored nest on the small rock/gravel bottom. Using a large dry fly like a **Stimulator** is a guarantee for fast action.

At other times, shoals attract smaller fish that seem to

be attracted by the relative protection of shallower water and the many small forage organisms that seem to grow nicely in these warmer and often highly productive waters. Predators will often patrol the edges of the shoal but are somewhat reluctant to move into the shallows during the day. In low light situations such as you might find at dawn or dusk, however, species like walleye and striped bass will make feeding forays into the shallowest water in an effort to get a quick meal. Use fish-like streamers and large aquatic invertebrate flies like crabs, crayfish and shrimp patterns. Cast first to the edge of the shoal and then if you get no response, cast up onto the shoal itself.

A smallmouth bass guarding its nest or redd.

POCKET WATER

When the current is running fast in a river, find some large rocks out in the flow. A large predator that does not want to fight the current sometimes will hide behind an in-river obstruction where the flow is less pronounced. Its attention is focused upstream and when it sees something to eat coming its way, it quickly enters the flow and tries to snap the morsel up. Whether successful or not, it then returns to its feeding position back in the low flow water to await the next feeding opportunity.

Place your fly into the pocket on the downstream side of the rock.

Because you are casting into or across fast water, your fly must get quickly to the fish's feeding zone. After a short moment the current is going to grab your fly line and create unnatural drag. If you are casting a dry fly, try to drop your fly into the pocket or just above it allowing the current to sweep your presentation into the slower moving water behind the obstruction.

Sometimes if I am using a weighted wet fly, I might even let it hit the rock and then fall into the pocket allowing it to quickly sink. Again, your fly won't stay in the feeding zone very long. The fish, however, is probably used to its prey moving quickly in this type of water so it may well be resolved to making rapid "*eat*" decisions. As soon as you complete your cast, quickly make the appropriate mend to reduce drag for the longest possible time and get line control. The take will be rapid and you don't want to miss it.

JETTIES, BREAKWATERS, GROINS AND BRIDGE ABUTMENTS

Fishing along a rocky shoreline in the early evening is a wonderful way to relax and catch a few fish for dinner.

Please be aware that fishing from any of these structures involves a bit of risk. The rocks can be very slippery especially if they are wet due to spray from a breaking wave. Bluegreen algae can almost look like dried oil on the most exposed rocks yet the smallest amount of moisture will turn the surface into a slick frictionless trap. Anglers and others venturing too near the water have fallen and some have even drowned.

All along our waterways, coastal engineers have designed all kinds of structures to stabilize our beaches and shore fronts. Some extend outward from the shore to protect or create safe harbors free from the pounding surf. Wave energy, which can be enormous, is dissipated as each wave breaks against and up the frontal surface. In most cases, there are spaces between the rocks or other materials used, and these spaces extend underwater all the way to the original bottom. Designers even expect some flexibility and movement to occur in the rocks to further absorb the oncoming wave energy.

Fish are attracted to all of these structures. As smaller animals inhabit the underwater crevices and surfaces and smaller fish take refuge in the spaces between the rocks, larger predators patrol along seeking any quick meal that they can find. Streamers, crab and shrimp imitations will generally serve you well as you cast out away from the structure or perhaps parallel to it. If there doesn't seem to be activity on one side, cross over the top and fish the other.

Predators, especially in the early morning or evening, will often chase baitfish into the cove created between the beach and the jetty or groin. If you are lucky in your time of arrival, you can cast safely from shore and won't even need to go up on the rocks. Landing a fish from shore, particularly one caught on a fairly light tippet, is just so much easier and safer too.

Jetties, breakwaters and groins provide excellent fishing locations but be careful of slippery rocks and wet surfaces.

Fishing at the mouth of a small navigational channel can often provide great results.

BACK EDDIES AND HOLES

As water flows downstream, it can be quite erosive and eat away at the left or right bank or even the river bottom itself. In time, a back eddy or hole can be created opening up another feeding opportunity for a predator. Holes are quite easy to fish because water is flowing downstream through them. Streamers, nymphs and dry flies are all good choices. Fish lying in the hole are waiting for food to come to them and because the flow rate decreases as it enters the hole, they have additional time to scrutinize your presentation before making the "eat" decision — so approach carefully and make your fly drift naturally.

Because the water flow is in the opposite direction in a back eddy, however, it can be a bit tricky to fish. Moreover, to add to the complexity, water flow from the main part of the river is still flowing downstream. So as you cast into the back eddy, your fly starts to travel in the upstream direction while your fly line moves in the opposite direction downstream. Within seconds and before your fly is able to fish the length of the eddy or even get to the desired fishing depth, it is sure to be dragged unnaturally downstream.

As one stream of water flows into the main river, look for pockets, holes and back eddies that will hold fish. Here a pocket of water is shown in the center of the photo.

One possible strategy to help you is to approach the back eddy from the same side of the river. Now at least you don't have to worry so much about opposite flow drag. I really like to fish dry flies and nymphs in eddies; and if I can fish from a downstream position, I usually can have a bit of fun and hook a few fish.

PLUNGE POOLS

Fishing into a dam's plunge pool is an excellent place to find feeding predators awaiting any disoriented prey.

Plunge pools below dams are excellent locations to find fish. The water is generally well oxygenated due to its fall from the top of the dam. Very often fish will merely swim around the pool and capture whatever prey is caught up in the somewhat turbulent water at the base of the dam. Sometimes in especially dynamic water flows, fish will hold closer to the bottom and wait for the opportunity to strike at a food item.

I like to use weighted flies in plunge pools as dry flies often just get lost in all the floating foam and bubbles moving about the surface. Here is a good time to use a tandem rig of two flies. The first can be a bead headed nymph and the second, trailing about 18 inches behind, a weighted **Woolly Bugger.** The nymph helps get the second fly down to a fishable depth. Another trick to get your fly down deep quickly is to cast directly into the waterfall at the base of the dam. Here, the water is flowing downward with some force and you are using its hydraulic energy to help carry your fly to deeper water as quickly as possible

FISH HAVE HABITAT NEEDS

To sum all of this up, remember that a fish lives in a given location because that area satisfies a matrix of habitat needs. For example, while some fish require shelter and cover, all fish have preferred spawning habitats, food preferences, oxygen levels, flow rates, water temperatures and water clarity. Some of the very best anglers know these needs well and use that information to position themselves or find locations where the species they desire to catch are most likely to be. Such spots may vary from season to season or even during various times of the day. Fish are able to move, and some do so quite often.

One general rule is that where you find an abundance of prey species, the predators won't be too far behind. Watch for concentrations of diving birds as they often indicate schools of prey being pressured toward the surface by predators. A fly angler will target the edges of the bait school or cast to its center and let the fly drop to a depth where the predators are lurking. Again, if you can match the hatch here by using a fly of the same approximate shape, silhouette, size, and color and make it behave as if it were a wounded prey, you will catch fish and often quite a few of them if you can only keep up with the fast-moving action.

Also, look for pinch points where a river may narrow or where a small river or stream enters a bay. If access is possible and the current is not too swift, locations such as these are often excellent. If fishing in saltwater, be aware that tidal flow may influence fish behavior. Many fish species will move into an estuary early on an incoming tide only to leave just as swiftly as the tide turns outward. Bonefish and stripped bass use this tidal feeding strategy almost daily.

Points or a collection of submerged or partially covered rocks are ideal spots to check out. Smaller fish often benefit from the protection and food opportunities these locations provide and larger fish are drawn to them for the same reasons. A well-cast fly to the edge of these rocks can often result in a beautiful fish for the wise angler who gets there early in the morning or at dusk as the predator moves in to feed.

The author holds a large rainbow trout caught at night.

Some predators like walleye and striped bass seem to be able to see better in low light than their prey. This gives them a distinct advantage that they exploit consistently to get a meal. Such predators may come into the shallows, where they are vulnerable to a fly, under cover of low light to seek and ambush a non-suspecting prey. An angler who gives up a bit of sleep may well be rewarded with a prize catch. Fishing under predator attracting lights at night can be a great strategy.

Successful bass anglers also will often fish drop offs where the bottom abruptly descends from a shallow area as well as any structure along an otherwise homogenous bottom. Using electronic fish finders, a bass angler will seek out these piles of debris, roots and stumps, rubble, rocks, or perhaps even a wreck. They know that all such structures can attract and hold prey — and where you find concentrations of prey species, predators won't be too far off.

Some fish like lake trout and smallmouth bass swim up to the shoals from their usual deeper haunts in the spring to spawn in relatively shallow areas. Look on bathymetric maps or navigational charts to locate these shoals and cast your fly first along the edges and then back onto them. I make this "edge first" suggestion because as soon as you catch the first fish, the commotion will likely alert other fish in the area. If you initially cast up onto the shoal and get lucky and catch a fish, you will then have to draw it back across the edge and disturb other fish that might have been closer to you. Disturbed fish go into a defensive mode and do not eat!

MUDS OR ROOTS

Some bottom feeding fish like bonefish form schools and feed together stirring up the fine bottom sediment as they progress along sucking and straining out edible crabs, shrimp or other small invertebrates. Not so unlike wild pigs that might root out something to eat, when the school becomes large these feeding fish can put so much sediment into suspension that the water appears cloudy. In stark contrast to the clear water nearby, the murky water easily can become as large as a football field. If you can detect the leading edge where the fish are likely to be and make a well-placed cast just ahead of them, your fly might be the next morsel a fish will grab.

A tidal flat is an excellent coastal location to catch fish. Clear and still water calls for slow movement and stealth. Polarizing sunglasses are a must.

SEAMS

A **seam** is a transitional area between waters flowing at different rates. Generally, a seam is created when faster moving water slides along a more protected and slower moving body of water. Predatory fish tend to align along the seam just outside the swift moving water.

Saving energy, these predators hold in the slower water ever vigilant to the approach of edible items carried in the swifter current. As a food item is recognized, the predator darts out to intercept it and then quickly retreats back to its preferred holding station. Since the fish are there to feed, all you have to do is pick the right fly and place it where it will drift downstream along the seam. I would go with a bead head nymph first and change to a dry fly if I see surface feeding activity.

Here there are three seams: one near the rock, one in the center and a third along the closest bank.

Fishing the seam along the side of swift moving water can often produce results.

CHAPTER

SEVEN

Common Fish Behaviors

At this point, you have balanced equipment and can deliver your fly with reasonable accuracy to a spot likely to hold fish. We can use the habitat information in the last chapter to show where fish are most likely to hang out. Now, let's explore some typical fish behaviors that can put a few things together and help you catch some fish.

After many years working as a Certified Fisheries Biologist, I have learned that fish are adaptive creatures. They exhibit a vast diversity of life style, form, size, shape and color. Fish have been around for about 450 million years. They have lived through ice ages and tropical climates. For a class of species to exist that long indicates that fish as a group are quite resilient.

Today's approximately 22,000 different fish species live in a broad range of aquatic habitats from very salty water such as the Salton Sea to eking out an existence under the ice in water as cold as 29°F. You can find greenback cutthroat trout living in lakes above 10,000 feet in Colorado and rattails and coelacanths at vast ocean depths. Blind fish have been found in deep caves and the snakehead of recent headlines can crawl about on land. The American eel is born somewhere out in the middle of the Atlantic ocean and migrates as a tiny transparent juvenile back to coastal rivers and streams where it grows to its adult form before heading back out to sea to mate. The giant blue fin tuna, highly prized by gourmet sushi chefs, migrate each year across many thousands of miles of open ocean. Indeed, the more we scientists learn about fish, the more we become amazed at what we don't know about this remarkable group of organisms.

Fish have developed all sorts of strategies to survive in a world filled with predators looking for a meal. Sticklebacks have spines which make them difficult to swallow, puffer fish blow themselves up to prevent ingestion, flying fish take to the air, eels can crawl overland, some species are poisonous and other species mimic them, some species might expel noxious chemicals or electrical shocks to ward off a would-be predator, some species that live in very deep waters use bursts of light to temporarily startle, distract or blind a pursuer. The list of defensive strategies goes on and on, allowing some fish species to populate nearly every water habitat on earth.

Though fish have made many adaptations to avoid capture, nevertheless there are some general fish behaviors that we anglers should know to help us catch them. Since we will be angling in lots of different habitats, one or more of these behaviors may come into play. Sometimes the solution is simple and at other times it is confoundingly complex. A good fly angler will learn and use typical fish behaviors to their advantage when the situation dictates just as a skilled golfer might need to assess a multidiscipline strategy when trying to sink a long putt across an undulating green. Let's review some of these behaviors and explore how we might use them to catch more fish.

FISH ORIENT UP CURRENT

While there are exceptions to every rule when it comes to fish, most sport fish have a shape that allows them to point efficiently into an oncoming water flow. An upstream orientation allows oxygenated water to pass easily over their gills to facilitate gas exchange. During its respiration process a fish absorbs oxygen and releases wastes like carbon dioxide. The fish merely has to hold its position in the current and all of its wastes are carried away from it.

Certainly a fish can, and many do, increase water flow across its gills by swimming.   Active swimming, however, requires work and this effort uses energy that also produces increased wastes. Resting on the bottom or even remaining stationary in a gentle mid depth current uses less energy than active swimming. A fish pointing upstream uses less energy and may not have to eat as much to live, grow and ultimately to reproduce. An actively swimming fish generally needs to eat more just to sustain itself.

A small school of coastal predators actively feeding on prey near the water's surface.

Probably the most important aspect of an upstream orientation is that on top of and within flowing water comes a virtual smorgasbord of things to eat. All a fish has to do is hold its position and wait for something edible to approach. If the item looks like something that might suit its tastes, the fish reacts to capture it using as little effort as possible. It may then return to its feeding station and resume its upstream vigil for the next morsel. Sometimes fish will set up behind some structural element like a rock or log where the current is quite minimal. Using even less effort, it waits for its next meal to flow its way.

It stands to reason, however, that the faster the water flow, the less time a fish has to react to eat something heading its way. Most fish prefer to have a little time to make the "eat" decision but competition with other fish may well modify that preference. The fish somehow knows that if it doesn't move quickly to eat the oncoming prey, some other fish may eat it first. Here is another reason why fishing where there are a lot of fish is a good thing!

Look where fast water approaches and enters a slower moving pool. Also, watch for any drop offs where the bottom abruptly deepens. Fish will often use these locations to feed on whatever morsel comes conveniently their way. On the salt flats or along a beach, you might actually see the target fish moving in one direction or another. If necessary to change location, move low, slow and stealthily. Ensure that the fish remains unaware of your presence. When you get into a position, make the best presentation possible. Cast far enough ahead of the fish so as not to spook it. If you do blow your cover, however, you may have to rest the pool for 10-15 minutes and give the fish a chance to resume its less defensive behavior before trying again.

Knowing that a fish is typically facing upstream should also help determine where to look to find a fish as well as how you might present your fly to catch it. Here is how I might go about it. First, as a common procedure, I would tie on a fly that matches the hatch or, at a minimum, make my best guess to match the size, shape, color and silhouette of what the fish may be feeding on at that moment. Again, I would be stealthy in my approach, moving quietly to get myself in a favorable position to make a cast upstream of the fish. It is key to get your fly centered in the fish's feeding lane or in a place where the fish is soon to go. You want the fish to see and be able to react to your fly so casting on top of or behind it is not a good thing. If the fish doesn't make the "*eat*" decision, your fly merely drifts downstream. Cast a few yards above where the fish is holding. If you are using a wet fly, the extra fly-to-fish distance will give you time to mend the fly line and also let the fly sink to about the same level that the fish is holding. Note that faster water may require you to cast even further upstream to allow greater sink time.

An upstream mend to the fly line will ensure a drag-free drift as the fly approaches the fish's **feeding window**, the area in front of a fish where a food item can be identified clearly and a decision made whether to eat it or not. Lastly, I would maintain good line control so that I might quickly set the hook if I feel the slightest tap to the fly line or see the fish move to take my fly.

SUBSURFACE FEEDING BEHAVIOR

It is an almost exclusive trait of freshwater species like trout, bass and bluegill to take flies floating on or above the water's surface. Meanwhile, remember that most fish spend most of their time feeding underwater. From your viewing position all may appear calm and peaceful. Several feet below the surface, however, a predator/prey drama is playing out constantly. Smaller fish, worms, crustaceans, squid, insects and other life-forms are being eaten. Sometimes the prey is being ingested quite violently. Bluefish, for example, commonly chop their quarry in half ingesting merely some of the prey, the rest to drift about to be picked up by a bird or some other fish that happens to be following the action. As we know from the Jaws movies, sharks can be particularly brutal as they flail a victim about trying to kill it by the most violent action it can exert upon the unfortunate prey firmly held by its many curved arrowhead shaped teeth. While it may not be pretty, sharks have to live too!

When the fish are down and not feeding on or near the surface, you just may have to go down to get them. Here you will use streamers, nymphs, scuds or other wet flies. When you don't know what the fish are feeding on, you may have to try several flies before you begin to get lucky. We call these flies **search patterns** because while we may target likely fish locations, we may not be certain that any fish are really there. Likewise, we are unsure of what they may be eating. We are probing hoping to get a strike while making a best guess on what fly might provoke a fish to bite.

In these situations be very aware of any subtle taps on your fly. You must keep vigilant for any hesitation in your fly line. Any atypical movement of your line or leader might well suggest a very subtle take. I have seen underwater videos clearly showing multiple takes of flies but because of angler inattention, the fish is able to spit the fly and resume feeding elsewhere. Above the surface, the angler is often oblivious to the subsurface action. While I don't advocate strike indicators because I am trying to teach good **line control**, I will admit that an indicator might improve the hookup rate of a daydreaming angler!

Good line control is a must. This means keeping a somewhat taught line between you and the fly by taking up slack in the fly line as the fly drifts down stream. The most common method is to raise the rod tip as the fly approaches you and then lower it again as it passes further downstream. If the target fish is upstream and in front of you, you can merely strip back excess fly line. Keep an eye for any underwater movement such as a flash or swirl near your fly. Sometimes these fish are very crafty so maintain concentration and be ready. With all wet flies, be prepared to strip set the hook should you feel or think a fish is mouthing your fly. At this moment, a short rapid strip of but a few inches is all that is needed to impale the hook into the fish's mouth. If you hook the fish, great; reel it in. In not, just continue to allow your fly to drift as you did earlier. As mentioned previously, where food is limiting relative to the numbers of feeding fish, competition among feeding predators may evoke a fish to strike when otherwise it would not. In Alaska, for example, I have seen fish race downstream to catch up with my fly before some other fish picks it up. When food is rare and summer is short, fish can surprise you with their aggressive feeding behavior.

SURFACE FEEDING

In many respects, fish feeding on or near the surface makes it easier on the angler. First, you have a really good idea of where the fish are. Second, the fish are in a feeding mode; they are looking for something to eat. Your difficulty is to figure out what is being eaten. If you quickly solve this puzzle, you are well on your way to catch a lot of fish. Here are some hints on what to look for.

As you watch the surface, are the fish making loud violent surface takes? Sometimes you can hear the "clump" as an air bubble is trapped in the back of the fish's mouth. Many times the fish will make a loud splash as its body breaks the surface or slams back down. I particularly love the way some trout and grayling leap from the water and grab my fly on the way back down. These exciting surface feeding behaviors suggest that you should be looking for the prey on or above the water's surface. In freshwater situations, look for any insects resting or skittering on top of the water. If possible, use a small fine mesh aquarium net to try to capture one. Having the bug in hand can confirm the size, color and shape of what the fish may be feeding. If you happen to capture multiple critters representing different species, your job will be more difficult but at least you have several possible patterns to try. With a bit of luck you might hit on the correct pattern right off the bat and be rewarded by catching some fish. If not, keep trying.

Sometimes you might see porpoising where the fish's back merely shows above the water's surface. The rise may be so subtle, you may not even be able to hear it despite being only several feet away. When you encounter these more gentle surface feeding behaviors, the fish are actually feeding by gently sipping at or just below the

This trout is waiting for the next morsel of food to drift its way.

surface film. The most likely form of prey would be an **emerger**. Emergers are insect forms that are transitioning from bottom lifeforms to adults that fly. Occasionally the aquatic form cannot easily break though the surface film and becomes vulnerable to being eaten. The view from underwater is of a fish methodically and gently sucking in these unfortunate prey.

In each case, the way a fish breaks the surface should give you an indication whether to use a dry fly or an emerger. Absent surface rises indicates that the fish are feeding elsewhere in the water column. Here nymphs and streamers are your best bets. The assumption is that a fish in a feeding station is actively searching for and feeding on typical food items that it sees and can react to capture. While it is not always the case, most fish cannot resist making minimal effort to eat something it knows to be edible. Your job as a fly angler is to present your fly into the fish's monitored feeding lane and make it appear like the item it ate a minute ago!

Like many anglers, when I arrive water side, I like to begin fishing right away — even if I don't know what food organism might be on the menu at that moment. As I approach the water, you can be assured that I am tuning in. For example, I am looking for any sign of predator or prey. Based on this early information, I might choose a wet or dry fly and fish with this pattern for the time being. Meanwhile, as I'm fishing, I am looking for anything that suggests a feeding predator. It might be a flash, splash or something even more subtle. I am constantly processing every bit of information I get and when I see something that suggests a feeding fish, I might change my fly to better take advantage of the current situation.

Even if you don't see anything, it tells you something. For example, remember that most fish are looking for something to eat almost constantly. If they are not feeding where you can see them, put your fly into a place where they are most likely feeding. Sometimes that means going deeper. Other times it means moving to a different spot that is more likely to hold feeding fish.

FISH WILL EXPEND ONLY SO MUCH ENERGY TO CAPTURE PREY

It is all about thermodynamics and energetics. Fish, like people and governments, can't perpetually expend more energy than they take in. Unlike Congress, nature does not run on deficit budgets. Fish, in order to grow, must actually take in more energy than they use. A rule of thumb in nature is that energy is reduced by a factor of about 10 when something is eaten. In other words, for every calorie the fish needs to live and grow, it must eat approximately 10 calories of food.

From an angler's perspective this is good because it means that fish have to eat a lot just to maintain itself. If they are to grow and reproduce, they have to eat a real lot. Oh, yeah! Now, where are my flies?

If you were to watch an underwater video of a trout in a feeding station, you would see that it moves only very short distances to capture something to eat. Generally, the faster the water flow, the less time it has to react and, as a result, the functional distance to get something decreases. In other words, fish move shorter distances to capture food in swift water. Another aspect of the same concept is that a fish is sometimes more willing to move a bit farther from it feeding station to capture a larger more calorically valuable food morsel. Conversely, if it is feeding on very small prey organisms, you can almost be certain it will not move about in swift currents a great deal. Rather, it will most likely hold fairly close to its preferred holding spot and move only to capture something directly within its feeding window.

The laws of energetics dictate that a fish or any other animal can only invest a limited amount of energy to pursue its food. At the end of the day if a fish is to grow, there must be a net gain of calories from all food sources. When prey is abundant, a fish might get a full stomach in a relatively short period of time. However, during times when food becomes scarce, things can get quite competitive. As an angler, you might really enjoy, at least for the moment, few prey and many predators. You are in a "buyer's market"! Unfortunately, however, this seemingly ideal situation might be short lived as predators might soon move on until they find new prey upon which to feed. If you can follow, great. If not, you sadly may watch some great fish move away from you and there may not be too much you can do about it. With luck and patience, the whole predator/prey dynamic might just come back in your direction — so be ready!

FISH PREFER CERTAIN WATER TEMPERATURES

While the ideal temperature among all fish species varies widely, a specific species may have a preferential range of only a few degrees. Some species will make seasonal migrations over great distances to stay in waters having their desired temperature range. Other fish make more modest movements within their respective basin by seeking out shallower or deeper areas as surface water temperatures fluctuate more broadly.

There is a small lake that I fish just after ice out in the spring. The water is still pretty cold yet the trout can be fairly active if you know where to go. By experience I have found that at one end of the lake there is a shallow section with a soft dark bottom. Here on a sunny afternoon, this area warms up faster than the rest of the lake. Fish find this area and become quite active as prey species also become increasingly active. I anchor my canoe just outside these warmer waters and by casting into the "hot zone" can catch quite a few trout. If you think about it, you may also know of similar conditions in your local waters. As you are out canoeing in the off season, keep these areas in the back of your mind for the coming spring.

Why is water temperature so important to a fish? We must go back to basic chemistry and biology to answer this question. Remember, for example, that fish are cold blooded which means that unlike mammals and birds that maintain a relatively constant internal body temperature, fish take on the approximate temperature of the water in which they swim. All of their bodily functions including digestion, respiration and reproduction are governed by body chemicals like enzymes and hormones. Without getting into too much detail, the concentration and the three dimensional shape of these chemicals is often slightly modified by temperature. It is the shape of the chemical that lets it do its job. Like us, if it is out of shape, which might occur in suboptimal temperatures, it just can't function as well as it otherwise might.

So, when viewed as a complex system, a fish's activity is greatly influenced by water temperature. Find a fish in its ideal temperature range and, for the most part, you will find a fish that is actively feeding. All of its enzymes and hormones are functioning optimally. Life in the fish world, at least at this moment, is good. When you come upon a group of fish in the middle of a feeding frenzy, you just can't tie your fly onto your line fast enough. Oh yeah, can you feel the urgency?

PREDATORS PREFER TO EAT AN INFIRMED OR DEBILITATED PREY

In nature, imperfection exists. Animals are born or develop conditions or infirmities that degrade their ability to keep up. These laggards become easy prey for a predator on a strict energy budget. While a fish is almost constantly seeking something to eat, it looks for something that appears to be slightly different than the rest. On a trout stream it might be an emerging insect that is struggling to climb out of its shuck or the outside shell that it used to cling to rocks on the bottom of the stream. In a saltwater bay, it might be something minor like an incomplete gill cover that exposes slightly more of the red gill. In both cases, a skillful predator can focus on such conditions and behaviors and target specifically the infirmed. In nature, if anything sticks out above the ordinary, something will usually come along and eliminate it. This is the law of the wild.

An angler, then, needs to at least consider making flies that match the hatch but may also include some natural like quirk that might give it some distinction among all the rest. This is especially critical when you might be fishing at a time when prey are remarkably abundant. Sometimes this might simply mean trying a fly that is slightly larger or a shade different than the natural. I like to introduce a little red color in some of my flies just to suggest to the fish a target for which they are already looking. If you give them what they want, you will catch a lot of fish.

SOME COLORS STIMULATE FISH TO EAT

As noted in the last paragraph, I think red is a color that fish focus on when they are looking for something to eat. Other anglers swear by chartreuse or orange. Purple has always been a preferential color of anglers seeking to catch largemouth and smallmouth bass.

While scientists know that fish see color, none of us really know how a fish processes that information in its very small brain. For example, while we know red is red, I am not sure what a fish perceives red to be below one meter as water absorbs increasing amounts of the light in the red part of the spectrum below this depth. I do know, however, that I catch a lot of fish well below three feet on my red headed **Woolly Bugger** and for that I am very thankful.

Streamers like the red and yellow **Mickey Finn** always seem to do well catching brook trout. Often these same waters will have populations of yellow perch so perhaps this popular fly mimics sufficiently a juvenile perch. Other colorful attractor flies, like a **Stimulator**, have ardent advocates within the angling community and I am sure that as you continue to develop in this sport, fellow anglers will provide additional tips on specific flies or color variations that have special meaning to them. In essence, it reaffirms that certain colors in certain waters can stimulate the interest of a fish and perhaps more selectively provoke it to chomp down on your fly.

MOVEMENT STIMULATES FISH TO EAT

There are two types of movement a fly can make that might provoke a fish to bite. The first is when some component or segment like legs, bristles or the tail of the fly moves. One of my favorite wet flies for early season trout is my red headed **Woolly Bugger**. To construct it, I use red thread, teal colored chenille, a long black chicken feather wrapped to give it bristles and, for the tail, olive marabou. When I really look at the fly as it is being stripped back toward me in rapid though short 2 to 6-inch herky-jerky pulls, I can see the palmered side chicken feather bristles pulsating back and forth in what might be construed to resemble leg swimming movements. Moreover, the movement in the tail is highlighted as each section of the tail reflects light in slightly different patterns along its length. To a fish, this would suggest a natural undulation it might commonly see in the tail of a swimming leech, fish, salamander or tadpole.

The other movement type of interest to predators include flee/escapes, hides and strange but natural behaviors. When a prey animal discovers it is being chased, it often tries to escape by swimming as quickly as it can away from the predator. If the predator has focused its attention to it as a specific target, the chase is on! I have been amazed to see as many as 8 to10 rainbow trout in hot pursuit of my fly. Is this great or what?

Sometimes if it perceives a threat, a prey species will seek shelter and try to hide. Small crabs and shrimp will do this on a Bahamian bonefish flat. If a bonefish sees the crab flee, it often will pursue it. The crab seeks shelter by quickly burrowing in the sand. The bonefish has seen this behavior before and immediately locks in on where it saw the puff of sand created by the crab. The bonefish puts its mouth over that spot and begins a suction process that it hopes will result in a meal of fresh crab. Substitute your shrimp imitation fly for a natural and I think you see the possibilities.

Sometimes prey are disabled either because of a developmental defect or, perhaps, by a wound from a previous encounter. Such conditions often cause the prey to behave awkwardly or at least not as fluidly as its peers. The condition creates strange but natural movements that set it apart from the rest. Predators love to focus in on any type of affliction that might allow it an easy meal. Unless it can find shelter where it might recover, the prey likely will become calories for the successful fish that eats it. Anyway, I think you get the point that if you get the right fly in the right color and make it behave in such a way that a predator will focus its attention to it, you will be successful in catching fish.

FISH DO NOT WANT TO GET EATEN

During the day and night, the main goal of a fish is to eat without getting eaten. They sure spend a lot of their effort to ensure this outcome. Sometimes they are successful. Nevertheless, far and away most fish ultimately get eaten by something. Very few fish die of old age and population success is achieved when two fish from each brood reach adulthood and spawn.

With so many of their siblings dying all around them, how is it that but a few fish actually survive? Perhaps it is just dumb luck. More than likely, however, similar to a successful stock market investor, those fish that do survive long enough to reproduce exhibit just the right balance of paranoia and greed. They want to eat as much as they can but they also must maintain an acute awareness of what is going on all about them during each and every feeding foray.

The faster and larger a fish grows might also provide it some measure of protection. A smaller predator may not be able to ingest it any longer. For example, some very large bluegills can live in the same waters as largemouth bass because they are bigger than the bass are able to swallow. The key, of course, in this strategy is to be able to get big quickly before something comes along and — gulp!

FEEDING SELECTIVITY

Over the eons, predators have evolved the ability to notice every microfacet of weakness exhibited by its prey. Witness how an Arctic tern dives into a school of bay anchovies or similar prey. The bird is not after the school but, before diving, makes a selection and targets a single fish. With some luck, the bird captures a meal and its chicks are fed. What did the bird see and react to? While we can only speculate, maybe it was a fish that was a bit bigger, or one of a slightly different color, or maybe an unfortunate individual that swam just a tad slower. Perhaps it was simply that this fish was closer to the surface than its peers. Whatever it was, something differentiated it from the rest.

In the chaos of a feeding frenzy what appears to be random carnage is actually the result of many rapid individual feeding decisions by each predator whereby a convenient prey is selected and chased. Target changes can be instantaneous, particularly if another prey becomes the "low hanging fruit." Nevertheless, there is a method to the natural madness where both the predator and prey have evolved together to ensure that no one species always has the advantage.

Predatory fish have similar abilities to the bird

mentioned above. While it may look like they are randomly plunging into a school of prey, in fact, predators are actually being very selective in their pursuit. As they move about the many, they are looking for some perceived weakness — some trait that sets this or that prey apart from the rest. Skilled in this ability, they can target select very quickly. When the determination is made, a successful predator focuses all of its attention on this one animal alone. If the predator is distracted by the confusion and flash of thousands of scurrying prey, it most likely will end the day hungry. For a predator, this is not good!

As a fly angler, you might be able to use some of this information to your advantage. When fish are surprisingly selective, they may well be expressing a behavior that keeps them from being caught. Over time and in locations with heavy fishing pressure, some fish learn that if they eat something and they have a positive outcome (like not getting caught), they will continue eating that item as long as it is available. The fish develop a sight pattern of that item and focus on eating objects that look, from their fishy perspective, pretty much as it ought to look. With an abundance of the primary targets available, anything else that appears to be different is avoided. Again, do not underestimate the skill of a fish to be aware of its surroundings or of its ability to see and hear extremely well.

Sometime you might be in the middle of a massive hatch with fish feeding all about you.   This can be quite exciting. It may well occur on a trout stream where various insects will be escaping from the water's surface in large numbers. You might hear a cacophony of splashes as trout slash the surface trying to catch as many bugs as possible.

With great speed, you search your fly box and come up with a fly that appears to match the hatch exactly. You make your best cast and now your fly becomes one of many naturals. Nothing. What is going on here? It can be quite frustrating not to catch anything in a seeming fishy wonderland. You may even be using low visibility fluorocarbon tippet. You are doing your part — now it is the fish's turn.

Keep watching the water because multiple hatches may be occurring and the fish may actually be feeding on something other than what you believe. A multiple hatch means that simultaneously several insect species are emerging from the bottom, rising to the surface, breaking out of their old skin or shuck and flying off to become adults. While your chosen fly may represent closely one of the insects, the fish are seeking quite another. Sometimes it might be a smaller insect or, perhaps, one of a slightly different color or shape.

Initially, stay with the same pattern or at least within the same size and color spectrum to see if your hookups increase. Still, don't waste too much time with one pattern that is obviously being seen and summarily rejected by the fish you are trying to catch. If your mechanics are correct, i.e.: your presentation and mending are giving you a drag-free float, your fly tippet connection is not visible, and your fly is consistently drifting into a known feeding lane, then perhaps it's time to change flies to a pattern that will be noticed by the predator and evoke some primordial urge to pursue and capture your fly — often in a most violent way. Patience now.

You know that the fish are eating. That's good! What you have to do is take a few more moments to determine what they *are* being eaten. Often these rises last for a short time so unless you figure it out quickly, you may very well be skunked. Short of actually pumping the stomach of a fish and examining its contents, here is where you must use all your observational skills to determine exactly what is going on around you. Guessing doesn't work! On last resort, if a friend is consistently catching fish and you are not, perhaps this might be a time to request assistance while offering to trade him your best hunting dog or at least tie him a dozen flies! Good Luck.

ADDITIONAL POINTS

Location in a pool: head vs. tail of pool. Actively feeding fish will often set up at the head of the pool just below a riffle. Here the water will have a higher level

Fishing upstream with dry flies is great fun. Proceed slowly. Watch for back eddies and holes that may hold fish. On windy days, consider using ant, grasshopper and beetle patterns.

of oxygen but foremost, the fish will have first access to any morsel of food floating downstream. Many times the younger and more aggressive fish will be stationed here. Meanwhile, the larger more seasoned fish will be in the middle or end of the pool waiting for the best feeding opportunities which might occur sporadically during the day or night. When fishing upstream to approach unaware from the fish's backside, I like to probe the downstream end of a pool first. From here, I move into the middle of the pool and then to the waters just below where it first flows into the pool.

Other fish feeding behaviors include solitary feeding.

Here one fish goes it alone. This behavior is most typical of the largest fish. They use selective pursuit, ambush, and even get below a school of baitfish and make occasional feeding forays into them only to retreat quickly back to safety of deeper water.

This angler has retrieved all the slack line and is fighting a large fish using the drag system of the reel.

Predators often practice group feeding behaviors where they hunt cooperatively with others of their species. Blue marlin, stripped bass, blue fish, walleye and other aggressive predators will relentlessly pursue prey. As the drama unfolds, the school of prey becomes tighter and tighter until they seem to swim as if they are one organism. From a predator's perspective, this might be quite good. Their prey are concentrated. The prey, being in a dense formation seem to be working together to flash, move and confuse. Many of them will survive to see another day. Nevertheless, others will not. This is the way of the often violent but natural predator/prey world.

CHAPTER

EIGHT

WHY A FISH MAY TAKE YOUR FLY

When you think about it, why would a healthy fish go out of its way to eat something composed of fur, feathers, metals and a myriad of synthetic components all tied together by the hand of man? Further, why would someone who is otherwise normal, go out into the water with a long stick, some fancy plastic line and toss the above noted object in the direction of where a fish might be? It just doesn't sound logical at all. Yet, hope springs eternal and each year about 12,000,000 of us do exactly that.

A float trip down a river can provide some exciting fly angling.

We are practicing the ancient art of deceit. The Trojan Horse, Eisenhower's cardboard armor and false airfield battle groups prior to D-day — all deceit! Using our guile and wit, we conjure all types of devices to make a fish believe something tied around our hook is good to eat.

So, for us, the smart ones, there is no hope. We go angling with the fly because we enjoy it. The fish, on the other hand, is just going about its daily routine trying its best to survive. Still, the question remains: what qualities embodied in our fly compel a fish to want to eat it? Like everything else in nature, this answer is not as simple as it might first appear. What a fish eats and even when it eats is generally defined by natural rhythms. Where a fish lives and when it feeds may not always be predictable but, through experience, we might be able to enhance our chances of locating a feeding fish. Perhaps if we better understand what might make a fish take our fly, we will begin to develop the insight we will need in selecting just the right fly pattern tied on the optimal size hook.

To increase our knowledge of fish and to help guide us to better fly selection, let's explore why a fish might want to eat your fly. In the section below, we will explore what makes a fly work.

10 Reasons why a fish may take your fly.

Flies work because:

1 ⟿ The fish is hungry and believes your fly is worthwhile to eat.

Somewhat like a South Beach dieter and without actually knowing, a fish is instinctively calorically aware. It somehow knows it's hungry and the only way to sate that hunger is to eat something. Going a step further, it can eat a few meals of high calorie rich foods like several smaller fish or it might select some lesser quality prey like small insects though it might have to eat many of them to gain the same number of calories. Fly anglers have a great advantage and, unlike other lure and bait fishermen, are not limited by the size of prey imitations. We can use flies larger than 6 inches and, a moment later, tie on an infinitesimally micro fly tied on a hook that we can barely see. Such hooks, all the way down to size 32 where more than a 100 might fit on the surface of a dime, can really challenge your eyesight just trying to thread the leader through its eye just to tie it on the end of your fly line.

Don't for a moment think fish are brilliant. I've heard it said that fish have an IQ of about two. While no scientist has ever measured absolutely a fish's brain power, a fish has about as much intelligence as it needs to survive and not much more. This is not to say that they are not wary and resourceful. Nevertheless, I have examined odd objects in a fish's stomach analysis like cigarette filters, hemlock needles, twigs, stones, and other unanticipated strange debris. Remember, a fish sometimes will eat anything it believes to be food. At other times, you just can't seem to buy a bite!

Basically, all we need to know is what the fish are feeding on now, and then try to match that food item as best we can. Sometimes this is not easy to discover but once the puzzle is solved and you begin to fish a reasonable imitation, your catch rate generally increases dramatically.

2—The fly resembles something that the fish is eating or has eaten before.

Fish do seem to have some memory or imprinting when it comes to food. They seem to remember prey and other food items that they have eaten before. I suspect, for example, that a fly tied in the shape of a trout pellet, a typical hatchery food, would work well on a recently stocked fish. A friend once told me that he would even toss a handful of small gravel into the water to simulate the sounds of hatchery food as it hits the water's surface. Deceitful, but it might work!

In a more natural setting, I've used successfully large mayfly imitations as long as two weeks after the Michigan mayfly (*Hexigenia*) hatch has passed. The fish have gorged on these flies for perhaps as long as a month during which time they build a strong imprint of what the food might be so even after the bugs are no longer naturally available, a fly that has the same color, size, shape and silhouette still provokes the desired "eat" response.

3—⌒The fly is conveniently in the right spot and at the right time.

Many fish predators are opportunists. If they were not, we would probably have a lot of thin undernourished fish! Some appear to be outright lazy, often waiting patiently for something edible to swim or drift within their **feeding window**. If deemed natural, the fish will strike, especially if they do not have to exert a great deal of energy to make the capture. The behavior is reinforced because the fish gets a net gain in energy for the amount of calories expended.

Most often, the fish will return to its favored ambush site to await the next food morsel headed its way. Some fish will defend vigorously these preferred **feeding lays** from the intrusion of other fish. The larger more aggressive fish stays while the smaller fish must seek its food elsewhere. This is why many small pools on streams with limited food flow hold perhaps just one larger fish. Note, while there may be several smaller cohabitating fish in the pool as well, these fish are for the most part actually feeding on something else and do not present a threat to the big fellow.

A successful angler will take advantage of feeding window/feeding lay opportunities by placing their fly, one that is common to the area being fished, just a few feet above the most likely fish holding spots. As the fly drifts naturally downstream it enters the feeding window and the opportunistic fish predator does what it is programmed by nature to do: strike!

4 — The fish is in an eating mode and is searching actively for food.

This is what fly anglers live for — to arrive at your favorite fly fishing waters and find fish actively moving about looking for something to eat. You might be able to see a fish sipping something here or there. Sometimes at dusk or the first thing in the morning when they don't have to worry so much about predators eating them, fish will patrol just below the surface in search of food.

To some extent, this is non selective feeding which means that you don't have to match any one particular prey species. Rather, you might have to guess what prey organisms might typically be available at that time. Terrestrials such as ants, beetles and grasshoppers are usually good dry fly starter imitations especially if the wind might be blowing just a bit causing these bugs to naturally fall into the water. At first light in the morning, a moth or other nocturnal bug imitation might also be a good pick to try. Sometimes these insects fall upon the water after an evening of mating or by mere accident.

Your first task, however, is not to spook the patrolling fish out of the feeding mode. Be patient and move slowly into a casting position. Try to get a handle on where the fish might be going and how quickly it might be going there. Watch for any surface or subsurface movements and try to predict when the next one might occur. When you make your presentation, make it far enough ahead of the foraging fish so as not to alarm it. If it doesn't know you are there, it most likely will continue on its feeding foray.

When the fish approaches the vicinity of your fly, often a small twitch movement of less than an inch or two will provoke a strike. If nothing happens after a short pause, initially and carefully lift the fly slowly from the water's surface so as not to cause an audible air pop, continuing to accelerate rearward, bring it to a full backcast and then relocate the fly to another likely spot. Meanwhile, always be alert as to what the fish may be feeding on. It just might be something smaller or perhaps larger than what you are using.

One hint is that if the waters you want to fish get a lot of angling pressure, you might try some real small imitations. Fish that previously had multiple hook ups after a while learn that only the smallest prey are safe to eat and will restrict their diet to the tiniest items they can find. Now, the pressure may shift to you because most angler's eye and hand coordination usually begins to fail rapidly with 7X tippet and size 24 hooks and smaller. Tying on these micro flies, especially in low light, really becomes the challenge!

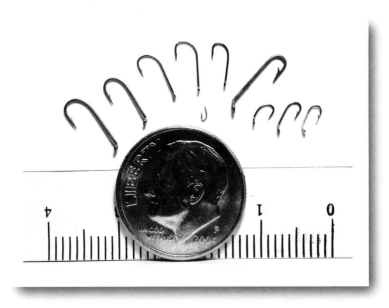

The Mustad Size 32 is the smallest functional hook ever made. For comparison, it is smaller than the ear on President Roosevelt on this dime reference.

5 — The fly behaves like something the fish has seen before.

Just as fish predators often behave in predictable patterns, their prey also behave in recurring ways. For example: caddis flies often skitter quickly across the surface; spawning mayflies seem to bounce about as they deposit their eggs; ants, beetles and grasshoppers seem to just struggle in place; small wounded fish tend to swim erratically; and hatching nymphs rise to the surface in a race to break out of their aquatic shucks, spread their wings and fly away before something eats them.

Each of these prey behaviors can be emulated to make your fly appear to be more natural. As I have mentioned before, fly fishing is an interactive sport. Unlike bait and bobber fishing, fly fishing often requires you to do something to make your fly appear to be alive. When fishing a caddis imitation, for example, the angler can strip a bit faster to make the fly appear to dance more quickly across the surface. Dappling the fly off the end of your fly rod (a technique that allows your fly to touch the surface for an instant, raising it into the air about a foot or two and then allowing it to touch the water once again), can mimic a spawning may fly. If a slow downstream drift doesn't work, another common technique when the mayflies are spawning actively is to make more frequent casts allowing your fly to touch the water for shorter periods.

Stripping back in erratic herky-jerky fashion your wet fly (a fly that sinks) can suggest to a fish predator a prey that is wounded or infirmed — an easy capture. When you observe certain prey behavior, try to figure a way to make your fly do the same thing. Quite often, the predator will respond in a predictable way and whack — fish on!

6 — Fly is in a position where fish expects it to be.

When a fish has been feeding in the same area day after day, it comes to expect food items to arrive in a certain way. For its little piece of the world, it gets to know just about every facet of ebb and flow. It knows what is natural and as long as a potential food item rests within prior encountered observations, the "eat" switch will turn on.

When fishing a dry fly (a fly that floats), I like it to sit high on the water. If you see a real bug on the water, its body often rests on its legs which, in turn, are being supported by the water's surface tension. The bug's body is actually slightly above the water's surface. Believe it or not, a fish looking for something natural to eat can make this subtle distinction. This is one reason why I use dry fly floatant prior to making my first cast. The treatment, pressed into the fibers of the fly, tends to repel and displace water allowing the fly to actually float higher on the water's surface.

Similarly, if the fish are feeding on emergers (insects that are changing from an aquatic lifeform to a free flying adult lifestyle), it might be more successful if some part of your fly actually exists on both sides of the water's surface just as the natural might. Here, to accomplish this, you might clip off some of the supporting bristles on the underside of your fly or maybe only treat the front half of the fly with the floatant material.

Sometimes on flat water you might see very small insects buzzing quickly just fractions of an inch above the surface and a fish occasionally raises its head in an effort to capture one. Note, the fish is focused on fast moving flying insects just above the surface. One trick that might help you catch that fish is to tie on a small fly about the size of the flying bug. Ensure that you have treated it well with dry fly floatant. Cast it in front of the foraging fish and just wait until the fish approaches the vicinity of your fly. When it gets close, make a fast 6 or 8-inch strip on the fly line. What you are doing is creating a small bow wave as the fly is pulled across the water's surface. If you time it right, the wave will be just a fraction of an inch higher than the surrounding water. Now, as the fly moves toward you, if only for an instant, it will rest on top of that wave about the same height above the water as the buzzing insect. The fish sees the bug right where it expects it to be and wham! Did I mention deceit?

7 —⌒Fly appears to be naturally free floating, drifting or moving … no drag or no tell-tail leader.

There are times when you want your fly to appear to be free floating. To be effective, it must move at the exact same rate as the water upon which it is floating. Any flow rate faster or slower will be a sure indicator to a wise fish that it is not a natural. If it is not a natural, it is to be avoided — no eat.

To get our fly to float naturally, we **mend** our fly line by adding an up stream arc to the fly line as soon as the cast is made. A mend allows the fly to drift more naturally for a longer period before the current accelerates your fly as the fly line is carried downstream much like the end of a whip might increase in speed toward the end of its forward or rearward cycle.

Another way your ruse to deceive a fish can come undone, is when your leader is detected by the fish. This happens several ways, the most common is when the leader is too heavy and it influences the freedom of the fly to float naturally. Another is when the leader is made from material that can actually be seen. Finally, if the leader rests on the surface without breaking through the water's surface tension, it can still leave a distinctive and perceptible trace causing the fish to go into a no eat mode.

Fortunately, each of these issues can be resolved easily. For example, the angler should always try to match the tippet size to the fly size as outlined earlier where the hook size is divided by the number 3. Although a bit expensive, fluorocarbon leader and tippet material has a refraction index near that of water which means that only a fish with

In situations where there is a strong downstream flow, make an upstream mend immediately after making a cast. This action will increase the time that your fly will drift drag-free downstream.

The Angler did not mend his fly line on this cast.

Do it correctly and you will be rewarded with a catch -- Fish On!

the keenest of eyesight will be able to see it. Lastly, your tackle shop should sell a product that when rubbed on the last few inches of you tippet just ahead of the fly, allows the tippet to sink below the surface and eliminates the telltale suspension of it on the surface.

Other factors that may alter the natural look of your fly include out of place fibers or feathers especially if they are wrapped around the bend of the hook. Another is having your hook fouled by algae or other debris — even if it is in minute quantities. The best practice here is to check your fly often to ensure that it is clean and ready to imitate your intended prey.

8 —◦Another fish appears to be interested in the fly.

Living in the natural world is very competitive especially if there is a limited critical resource and the one driving resource of all predators is the ongoing need for food. When food is relatively scarce, fear and its associated withdrawn behavior become less important. If a fish hasn't eaten in a while, it becomes willing to accept greater risk. It expresses this behavior by moving about more widely, being more observant to food opportunities, becoming more aggressive in its pursuit of prey, or being active during parts of the day when it normally would be resting.

In my analogy of fish with regard to feeding, I often relate it to a binary on/off switch.   When a fish predator sees a potential food item, it must decide: eat or don't eat. When food is scarce and a potential food item appears, the fish is more likely to make a decision to eat.

Now, let's take this one step further and place that predator among several of its peers. If one of the fish first spots a prey, it may hesitate (the fear factor) for a millisecond. Meanwhile, a hungrier more aggressive fish nearby also views the prey and instantly and instinctively initiates an attack. The first fish which was kind of sitting on the sidelines now is reassured that the food is a natural and if it doesn't act quickly will loose out. The eat switch is turned on as both fish address a compelling urge to get to the prey first. In this case, the second fish's aggressive feeding behavior helps sway the first fish to an eat decision as well. Remember, fish predators are inherently greedy and don't want to be left out when it comes to eating prey.

Competition, however, can sometimes work against you. For example, you might have a problem if you are fishing for a large trophy fish or perhaps trying to catch a particular target species but your preferred catch is mixed in with numerous individuals of another more aggressive fish species. Here we might encounter a situation where the smaller fish will attack your fly while the older veteran lingers back. In order to catch the big fellow, you may well have to catch some of the smaller fish first.

Recently, I was fishing on the Beaverkill River in New York and the legendary fly fishing diva Joan Wulff stopped by to watch. I noted a mayfly rising from the water and tied on a likely imitation. Meanwhile, I was carrying on a friendly conversation with Joan and her husband Ted. As luck would have it, a fish came up and hit my fly but since I was distracted, I missed setting the hook. Roars from the gallery went up as to why I missed the fish. Distracted again, I missed another opportunity to set the hook when a second fish rose for my fly further downstream. Now, the roar was really blaring! Undeterred, I then lifted my fly and repositioned it upstream of where I just missed the first fish. Concentrating now, I watched the fly drift into the feeding window and was rewarded when a big lunker brown trout rose up to take my fly. I didn't miss this time and the gallery cheered! After releasing my beautiful prize, I cut my fly and gave it to Joan for her use the following day. My reason, I explained, for missing the first two fish of course was that I was trying to catch the big boy and just needed to clear the little fellows out of the way!

Another example that comes to mind is that in certain streams in Alaska, grayling abound. When a friend asked me how to catch the fewer rainbow trout mixed in, I suggested that he might have to catch and release all the grayling first.   In fact, this is what had to happen. The rainbow trout were not as speedy or aggressive as the grayling. However, when the grayling were removed from the competition, the slower moving trout then had opportunity to take the fly. They did and my friend caught his rainbow!

9—Fly appears to be trying to escape or hide.

Predators almost always will react toward a flee response from a prey. When some prey organism is trying to flee a predator, it will exhibit certain provocative behaviors that turn the fish's eat switch on. Predators want to eat something natural and these behaviors indicate to them that the prey is, indeed, natural and worthy of pursuit.

One typical prey flee behavior besides outright swimming in the opposite direction involves escaping into the air. Note that smaller fish often burst from the water into the air when they are being hotly pursued by aggressive predators. Sometimes the prey is successful in its escape but occasionally the predator in a very exciting and spectacular exhibition takes to the air as well. Casting your well matched fly into this kind of mix can very often result in fantastic action.

Another flee behavior is when the prey tries to hide. When a bonefish is foraging, crabs and shrimp will often make short swims before trying to settle into the bottom and hide under the sand. The bonefish recognizes the fleeing motion as well as the puff of sand disturbed as the prey seeks protection in the bottom sediment. With its hard cartilaginous subterminal mouth over the most likely hiding spot, the bonefish is ideally suited to exert considerable suction while filtering out the prey from the sediment.

In freshwater habitats, an insect emerger is in a race to shed their **nymphal shuck** (its aquatic exoskeleton or shell) and fly off the water's surface to begin another phase of its complex life history. Fish come to learn that the emerger is vulnerable from the time it leaves the security of the bottom until it secures its new perch on a riparian bush or tree. At the water's surface, it must break free from its old shell, unfold its new wings and escape into the air before something comes along and eats it. Although this is a common occurrence in nature, it is by no means easy and lots of things can go wrong. The predator is there to gather up any insects it can and particularly those that may be having more of a struggle.

The drama continues to unfold as the adult form of the insect is set to begin to fly.   The fish instinctively knows that if it doesn't act quickly, it will miss a feeding opportunity.   The bug makes its last struggle to free itself from its **nymphal shuck** and the fish reacts to that movement.   Many times the bug will win and flies safely to a nearby bush.   Nevertheless, the fish will eat others and over the course of the day will get enough to sustain itself and reinforce a feeding behavior that targets emergers as they undergo a metamorphosis into flying adults.

10. Fly looks or behaves differently from any prey it is made to resemble.

A friend related to me that on a recent fishing trip to Maine, he initially was unable to catch any fish despite an ongoing hatch. He used a fly that had all of the same size and color characteristics of the prey but still did not get any hookups. When he tried the same pattern that was slightly larger, he began to have success. What he did was to make his fly more distinguishable.

This "set apart" technique often works with attractor flies like yellow and red humpies and, perhaps the best attractor dry fly, the **Royal Wulff** (as discussed in chapter 3). These patterns don't really resemble anything natural and common to the area being fished. However, because they look or act differently from most prey that a predator would normally encounter and yet still have some characteristics of being natural, curiosity or some other primal urge is evoked and the eat switch is turned on. The point here is that if conformity doesn't work, you might have to become a contrarian to achieve your objective and catch fish.

Smallmouth Bass taking a Bead head Hare's Mask Nymph.

CHAPTER

NINE

WHY A FISH REFUSES YOUR FLY

In Chapter 8 we learned why a fish might take your fly. In this chapter, I will outline for you some of the most common reasons why a fish will look at your fly and then just as quickly, decide that it is not something it wishes to eat at that moment. Having a handle on this obverse information should help you better diagnose those situations when you can't seem to even buy a bite.

It will happen and there will be days when you go fishing and the fish just won't bite. Other anglers about you may prognosticate and blame the weather, wind direction, too warm or too cold, too much sunlight or too little sunlight, no fish, and the list goes on. I will assume that you are fishing in waters that indeed hold fish. If that is the case, you might ask a very legitimate question. *So what actually may be happening and why am I not catching fish?*

This can be very frustrating but that is why it is called *fishing* and not *catching*. Outlined below are some common reasons to help you understand, despite all of your efforts, why a fish still won't take your fly. Sometimes it may just be one thing and at other times it might be several perplexing factors at play. Perhaps this discussion might help you sort it out and let you begin to catch fish once again marveling your nearby angling pals!

A smallmouth bass.

10 Reasons why a fish won't take your fly:

1 — Fly resembles something the fish does not want to eat.

When a fish is focused on eating something else, it doesn't make much of a difference what you throw at it. In these situations, you really have to use all of your observational prowess to get every clue on what the fish are eating. Sometimes, it is just not easy particularly when you are fishing at the end of the day and running out of daylight. One time several years back I was fishing on the upper Delaware River with some friends. Despite several hatches occurring that evening and feeding fish all around, none of us caught many fish. Obviously, we were not giving the fish what they wanted.

Taking the optimistic view, we can be fortunate that this level of fish feeding selectivity doesn't often occur. Another thing in our favor is that selective hatches usually are short lived transitioning naturally to a different hatch perhaps within an hour or two. If decreasing daylight is not a factor, your persistence and patience will be rewarded if you can just hang in there. Meanwhile, don't be married to one fly pattern. Use this time on the water to try different flies. You might even tie on that one fly that didn't quite come out right but you threw it in your fly box just in case. If for no other reason, tying on different patterns gives you something to do while you are enjoying the sights, sounds and smells associated with an otherwise pleasant evening. Finally, when you do get together with your friends later for an after action discussion, you can all exchange stories about what you tried and the various strategies each of you used. Over a cup of coffee and a nice donut, these interactions with friends make for wonderful fellowship.

2—Fish can see or hear you and, by experience, knows your fly is not a natural.

I mentioned earlier about stealth when approaching feeding fish. Remember that sounds can travel much faster and farther through water than through air. If you startle a fish, it will go into a no eat mode immediately. It may stay in fear for a short time or perhaps as long as an hour. While it may vary greatly between species, in general I use about 10 to 15 minutes as how long a fish might take to resume its normal feeding behavior. Of course there are exceptions for this rule of thumb, but resting a pool or letting things quiet down for a short time might not be a bad idea in some cases.

Once I was in a small backwater stream in Alaska. I caught a grayling and then gently released it. Since the water was clear and there were few fish in that backwater, I watched with amazement when that fish within moments of release return to its former feeding station and resumed feeding — probably within 30 seconds of having been caught!

Another rule that I use is if you can see the fish, it is likely that the fish can see you.   Further, if the fish can see you, it knows that whatever else you are doing, it likely will not benefit the fish. Even if you make a great presentation with a superbly matched fly, the fish may well associate your presence with danger.

Remember that from a fish's perspective since birth just about everything in nature wants to eat it. It probably has had many close calls from fish eating birds like great blue herons, terns, gulls, pelicans, ospreys, and eagles. Similarly, it has been pursued underwater by a host of larger fish and fish eating mammals like otters, mink, seals and bears. If it is to remain alive, it must be alert to any and all threats, so while it doesn't exactly know that you are a human, it still needs to treat you as something that may want to eat it — or at least catch it.

3—Fish can detect leader and heavy landing fly line.

We discussed tell-tail leaders and their impact on skittish fish in the last chapter so here we will address another associated problem. Note that if a fish detects a leader or a fly line, it may very well stop feeding. Seasoned anglers use a term called **lining the fish** to indicate that the line has been cast over the top of a fish. This can really be a problem when fishing upstream when you are not exactly sure where the fish may be holding. It can also be an issue when fishing on a salt flat when fish like permit and bonefish are on the move and heading perhaps in your direction. You might inadvertently cast too far and as a result, your fly line falls just above them.

Most weight forward fly lines, especially those designed to handle larger saltwater fish, have fairly large diameters. No matter how careful you cast them, they often will land on the water in less than a delicate fashion. Sometimes the body of your fly line will make an outright splash while the fly at the end of your leader may land ever so lightly upon the water. While you may be concentrating on the fly, if that splash is over the top of or quite near the targeted fish, an alert that something unnatural has occurred could spook the fish. Fish do not regularly see fly line, especially those with bright outlandish colors, fall from the sky coming to rest on top of them.

A couple of suggestions to help you in these situations is to buy fly lines that have natural colors like tan, green, blue or clear. Here, you won't have an odd fly line color give away your position. Next, if you can see the fish, cast slightly off to the left or right, preferably in the direction that the fish may be heading. Thirdly, if you are not quite sure exactly where the fish maybe holding, cast short first and then work subsequent presentations to probe more distant likely fish holding spots. Finally, you may wish to use longer leaders.

4—Fish is more interested in mating, nest building, finding a mate or discouraging a rival.

Over time I have come to learn that fish involved in courting, mating or reproductive behavior have little or no interest in eating. I've watched two male fish chase each other here and there and around in circles to discourage the other from having the opportunity to mate with the desired female. Enticing a nesting fish to your fly can, at times, also present a challenge. Obviously, these fish have something else in mind.

There are a few things that you might do, however, to improve your chances. For example, we know that one male tends to be aggressive to all other potential suitors. Some fish, common in trout and salmon, develop mature male sexual abilities when relatively young and thus much smaller fish. While the larger males have the ability to stimulate a female to begin shedding her eggs, the smaller males, called precocious parr, can intervene at the opportune moment of the sexual process and fertilize some of the eggs. This can be very irritating to the large male. Now, visualize a fly dressed to mimic one of these smaller male fish teasing the larger male. Instinctively, the larger fish will snap at your fly, not because it wants a meal but rather much the way you might swat at an irritating fly or mosquito.

Another example involves returning salmon. In Alaska a few years back a fellow taught me an interesting trick. He was using a fly that resembled a small shrimp. The fellow's explanation was that the fish has for a few years been out in the ocean routinely eating these small crustaceans. The reactive behavior to snap at these prey is so well learned and ingrained that the salmon still continues to exhibit the feeding behavior even though it is on its upstream migration and no longer needs nor desires to feed.

The above examples demonstrate that even if the fish are not eating, a strategy might be devised to take advantage of what the fish might be doing. The key to your success is to remain undetected. Meanwhile, you can observe the fish's behavior and then figure out why it might be acting that way. The last piece of the puzzle then is for you to develop a technique that will provoke the fish to lash out after your fly.

5—Fish has become ultra selective on a specific prey species.

Face it, there are going to be times that the fish are going to be so selective that only imitations precisely emulating the prey in size, color, shape and silhouette will hook fish. In some slower moving ultra clear eastern freestone creeks, trout can be particularly persnickety. If there is a local fly shop nearby, the shop owner might be able to help you select a few flies that could help you through these difficult situations. Also, you might meet an experienced fellow angler who is willing to share their success with you.

In lieu of these fast track routes to success, if you can

capture the suspected prey in a fine mesh aquarium net, you might be able to tie a fly yourself that successfully imitates what the fish are eating. Some anglers who have been lucky enough to catch one fish have been known to use a stomach pump to suction a fish's stomach to determine what a given fish has eaten. With this information at hand, they can go through their fly inventory to see if they have something approaching the natural food. Of course, the fly tying option is always a possibility if you remembered to take your fly tying kit along on the trip.

The above suggests an excellent example where several years ago a group of friends were fishing in Argentina. When one angler observed a very small caddis was having success, everyone scurried to see if they might have similar flies with them. When none was found, one of our pals went back to the vehicle where he had his vise and materials. An hour later, he came back and gave each of us one of the flies he had just tied. Now, thanks to this wonderful and selfless gesture, we all were catching fish. You see, sometimes good fishing is not all about catching fish!

6 — Fish is resting or in a non-eating mode.

Every once in a while you may encounter fish just lying on the bottom apparently resting.   I mean you can see the fish — sometimes more than one — holding fairly quietly in the same location. You approach them slowly and with caution. You make that great cast with what you believe to be the right fly — nothing. You change flies and again make a perfect presentation. Again: nothing. You change flies again and yet again. What is going on? You ask yourself, what am I doing wrong?

Relax, it may not be you or your selection of flies after all. The fish, for lack of a better description of their behavior, may be resting. They also may be preoccupied with some unperceived threat, or, perhaps with their stomachs full from an earlier eating binge, they merely may be digesting the food. If the water temperature is cold, a fish's metabolism will also slow meaning that it may not need to eat as often. Another possibility is that the fish may be anticipating a hatch that consistently occurs about the same time each day. Lastly, they may be waiting for a time of day when because of diminished daylight, they can feed more freely without being so exposed to larger predators.

There are also times when a fish is constrained by suboptimal habitat such as may occur during the summer. Here, warmer, less oxygenated water, may surround the cooler more preferred water from a spring seep. Fish may hold quietly in these smaller habitats so as not to attract attention from other predators seeking a meal.

7 — Fish is migrating or intent on moving elsewhere.

Fish are quite mobile and commonly move from place to place. Fish, for various reasons, will move from deeper water to more shallow habitats and then back again. Beside up and down forays, lateral fish movements can be quite modest amounting to several hundred feet or more as the fish go about their daily routines to forage for food or seek protection.

Some movements like seasonal migrations, however, may exceed many hundreds of miles. While these fish may be seeking waters having preferred thermal qualities, more than likely they are pursuing prey species that are also seeking water with comfortable temperatures. The net effect is that both predator and prey move from place to place as the seasons progress.

Still again there are times when a fish's priority shifts from the pursuit of food and initiate large scale migrations for purposes of reproduction. The classic example of this is the well known runs that occur when after one or more years at sea salmon, shad, and herring return each year from the open ocean to coastal rivers. The fidelity of these fish to their natal streams is remarkable.

What makes a fish move from one location to another may well determine if the fish is in an eating mode or not. If the predator is actively seeking prey, you may be in luck. If they are motivated by a primal reproductive urge, lack of immediate interest in food and the opportunity to capture prey may make your fly presentation less appealing. Nevertheless, anglers have had considerable success when they entice a fish to the hook by making it angry or even presenting a fly that reminds it of something it has eaten so often in its recent past thereby evoking a strike out of habit. In both cases, you win!

Locally, as what might occur on a salt flat, if a fish is headed off in one direction, there may not be much you can do to get it to alter course. It is even more unlikely to alter the movement of a group of fish because these fish are reacting collectively to the directional movements of the group. Unless you can get your fly in front of one of the school's leaders, hoping that one fish will leave the security of the group and alter its course to chase your fly may be wishful thinking. Nevertheless, what have you got to loose? Go ahead and make the presentation as best you can. You never know, the whole group may abruptly turn back and head right for your fly.

There are also times that experienced anglers will set up in well-known locations where groups of fish have been known to pass. Such pinch points can be the narrows between two islands or channels between two lakes or bays. In these examples, fish movements may be influenced by tide, time of day or, perhaps, seasonal changes. The angler merely has to wait, remain vigilant and, if well positioned, the fish will come within casting range. Whether or not these migrating fish take an interest in your fly can be a challenge to your patience and skill. Remember, their main urge may well be to get to another place and feeding on available prey may not be as compelling to them as you might wish.

8 —◌ Fly looks or behaves unnatural.

After a fly leaves your hand and sails through the air in any casting sequence, something unintended may happen to it that reduces its ability to look natural. If the fly is imbalanced or has tail fibers wrapped around the hook's bend, it will not appear to be natural. Similarly, if there is a bit of weed, scum or other debris fouling the hook, a fish will see it as something that is not quite right and let your presentation pass by unscathed. Obviously, this is not your intention so every once in a while, bring in your fly and check it for anything that might possibly alter its ability to look natural.

In addition to fouling, perhaps the biggest turnoff for a fish is **drag**. When a leaf or a piece of underwater debris flows downstream, it flows at about the same rate as the nearby water that surrounds it. This is natural. On the other hand, should your fly flow at a faster or slower rate than the waters proximate to it, a visual cue is established suggesting that your fly is not natural. Fish are the ultimate organic food consumers and those that have learned to survive eat natural stuff and avoid potential foods that appear unnatural.

After you present your fly onto moving water, it will for a while drift naturally. Meanwhile, your fly line will also come to rest on the water as well. Now as the downstream current encounters and begins to pull your fly line downstream, your fly initially drifting at water's flow rate will begin to accelerate increasingly much like the knot at the end of a bull whip. Accelerating flies that move at whip like speeds do not generally evoke a fish to strike.

Anglers that have learned how to mend a fly line effectively can minimize drag enabling their flies to drift downstream naturally for longer periods. Remember the words of my grandfather who told me that if you want to catch a fish, you have to have your fly in the water.

The more time that your fly drifts naturally, the more opportunity you have to entice a fish to attack your fly.

9—Fish may have learned the pattern — perhaps it was caught on the same fly previously.

There have been times when I am out fishing that it seems so easy. I make a cast and catch a fish. Cast after cast yields yet more fish. It is at times like these that I might well change flies putting my successful pattern aside to try something else. I use this strategy particularly when I might be back in these very same waters in the next day or so.

Similarly, when I am going to be fishing a relatively small pond or lake, I might not give my most successful pattern to someone that will be fishing there a day or two before I get a chance to fish said lake. In both cases, I am concerned that the fish will learn my fly and then avoid it.

Fish can and do learn from being caught. While they may not have a lot of brain power, some species seem to have limited memory of what is natural food and what isn't. If you sting every fish in the pond with a given fly, you can be assured that on your next trip to that pond, particularly if it is in a matter of days, that same pattern won't be as successful.

It also follows that if you are going to fish an area that receives high and constant fishing pressure, you generally will have to fish smaller flies, sometimes quite small, or patterns that more precisely match the current hatch.

10—Poor fly placement where fish either doesn't see it or has to move too far to get to it.

There have been times when I cast my fly and it alights on the water and out of nowhere a fish will come to slam it. I have seen fish rushing back down river to catch up to my downstream drifting fly before another fish is able to capture it. This example is more indicative of a place with a shortened season or fairly low productivity. The fish have to capture every calorie they can when available. Selectivity, when it comes to food, is not as important as gaining as much food as possible in the shortest amount of time.

Of course, this is not the norm. Typically we anglers are confronted with far fewer actively feeding fish and even those fish exercise some moderate degree of fly selectivity. If our presentation is not quite right and we deliver the fly beyond the fish's feeding window, no matter how well we mend the fly line we are not likely to catch that fish. It really all comes down to if you want to catch a fish, you have to understand better where the fish is likely to be and deliver your fly, one that has a reasonable chance of provoking a strike, to a location where the fish is expecting its food to be.

As you increase your fly fishing experience and you catch more fish, try to remember where you placed your fly and where the fish first struck it. Over time, you will build an inventory of likely fish holding habitats and when you enter a new river, stream, pond, lake or bay, look at the current habitat for similarities and familiar haunts and reflect on where you have caught fish in the past. Try to think: "if I were a fish, where would I be?" Use all of these skills to probe likely locations and remember that most fish are unlikely to move any appreciable distance to take your fly. As an angler, your job is to get the fly to them without giving the fish a clue that you are, indeed, a threat.

CHAPTER

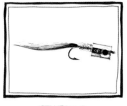

TEN

WRAP UP

Fly fishing from a low canoe is not so unlike fly fishing from a wheel chair. The arm motion and the distance above the water are about the same.

Before we finish up, let's go over a few key fly fishing principles. First among these is that you don't need an extensive inventory of flies to catch fish. I highlighted 24 fly patterns that, if used with confidence, will catch a lot of fish for you — almost anywhere in the world! As you become more experienced in the sport, I am sure you will add more flies to your collection. Nevertheless, these 24 patterns will take you a long way.

For those experienced fly anglers who may be reading this, I hope you will agree with most of my choices or at least appreciate why I selected a given pattern. I also challenge you take a few moments to assist a novice fly angler who may not be as successful catching fish as you. Remember, everyone benefits when someone new to our sport learns the importance of quality waters, quality fish and quality habitats. It all begins with quality experiences and your simple gesture of help might mean all the difference.

At the beginning of the book, I introduced a series of flow diagrams to guide you through fly line and fly selection. If you follow the charts and answer each question, you will have a pretty good head start in tying on just the right fly. After all, these are the same questions seasoned anglers, myself included, ask themselves when they approach an unfamiliar stream, river, pond, lake, or bay. Be patient with the fly you selected. Give it a fair chance to perform for you. Alter your retrieves or perhaps move a short distance to another likely fishing spot. However, if after a reasonable try, don't hesitate switching to one of the alternative patterns in your effort to entice a fish to strike your fly.

I also discussed each of the recommended fly patterns and offered color and size preferences where appropriate. In time, you may wish to explore other colors and sizes. I also provided a brief summary of the origin of each fly as a way of introducing you to the long tradition of fly fishing. I believe that fly fishing represents an important and growing component of recreational fishing and I want you to be a part of this heritage.

A fly will most often catch a fish in the lips and boney mouth parts resulting in minimal danger to vital areas.

Research shows that a fish caught on a fly and then released has a high likelihood of being alive 24 hours later. All anglers enjoy catching fish and many fly anglers now release almost all of the fish they catch. They get to experience the thrill of the catch yet are able to release safely the fish for someone else possibly to catch later on.

The 24 recommended flies represent five overall pattern groups including Drys, Nymphs, Streamers, Attractors and Emergers. Each group suggests a category of prey species likely to provoke a fish to want to eat it. Some of these flies can be fished on the water's surface and some can be fished submerged. Some patterns can be equally effective on or under the water depending on your situation. I encourage you to experiment to see what might work for you. If the way you fish a fly is successful, repeat whatever you did and see if you can get some consistency.

With dry flies, you might consider using one hook size larger west of the Mississippi. Western rivers, especially those with steep gradients, flow a bit faster and larger dry flies generally can be seen better by both you and the fish.

In salt water, use corrosion resistant hooks and after use be sure to rinse thoroughly your rod, reel and your flies in freshwater. As with all flies, be sure they are well dried before you put them back into your fly box. Hooks will rust and rusty hooks while not stay as sharp may also become brittle. I like to use waterproof fly boxes as I occasionally drop the box into the water. With my old fly boxes, I had to take all the flies out, dry them and then put them back.

Most predators feed below the surface most of the time. For this reason, if you don't see signs of surface feeding, don't hesitate to tie on a sinking fly. Meanwhile, keep your eyes open for any change in predator feeding behavior. Sometimes it will be very subtle and at other times explosive. Be prepared to switch to a different pattern should circumstances change.

When you tie your fly onto the tapered leader or tippet, be sure you use a strong and secure knot. All knots are not equal and most knots reduce the breaking strength designed into the line by the manufacturer. Use water or saliva to lubricate the tightening of the knot. This simple action also cools the line friction as it is being drawn tightly into the desired knot.

Pay attention to balance when putting together you fly fishing outfit. If your gear is out of balance, you may have problems and get frustrated. An unbalanced rig will also get you tired sooner and contribute to wayward knots being tied in your fly line. The one exception to help you better feel the casting motion is to use a fly line rated one weight size larger than the rod rating. Remember, you are there to have fun and frequently stopping to untie knots can be a real drag. Casting a balanced fly rod is not so unlike listening to a tuned musical instrument — sweet!

A happy angler with a bag limit of bright red salmon.

If you practice your casting and can deliver a fly to a spot, you are well on your way to success. I generally ask my students to be able to cast 30 feet of fly line beyond the rod tip.   I do this for several good reasons. First, I want them to be able to cast to a small defined area — the spot. Second, fly line manufacturers generally put most of the weight in the first 30 feet of weight forward line so it should be easy to cast that distance. Next, if a 9-foot leader is being used, the angler is delivering the fly 30 feet plus 9 feet or 39 feet beyond the rod tip. Now, if a 9-foot fly rod is being used, the fly is actually 48 feet from the angler. Quite impressive!

These are relatively important dimensions because as light refracts differently in water and air, a fish underwater is unlikely to see an angler standing waist deep in water beyond 30 to 35 feet. If your fly is reaching the fish 48 feet from where you are standing, it won't see you. So, if you are stealthy in your approach (remember sound travels much farther underwater), the fish won't suspect that you are there and will continue to feed as it normally would.

Knowing why a fish might take your fly as well as some of the turn offs gives you a perspective of an accomplished angler. Good practices will always swing luck in your favor. Bad habits, on the other hand, will reduce any edge you might have. By learning what might turn a fish on and off will better equip you to approach and understand each unique fishing situation encountered.

A key to catching fish is knowing where to look for fish. As you come upon a new water, try to identify typical fish habitats. Think like a fish — that is, if I were a fish, where would I be? Fish are where they are for a reason and generally that reason is because food is available for them to eat. Feeding fish are much easier to catch. Exploit that fact by stealthily fishing in these key habitats, use one of the suggested fly patterns and deliver your fly to a place where the fish can see it. Make it look and behave as if it were a natural prey. Do these things and you are very likely to catch fish — a lot of them!

BE THE FLY!

A neat way to carry your daily bag limit.

GLOSSARY

Drag   Unnatural drift of a fly downstream normally created when the water's current bears on the fly line. As a result of the fly line's drag, like the end of a whip the fly accelerates faster than the natural water flow.

Feeding window/search window   The area above and ahead of a feeding fish is scanned continuously for oncoming food. Faster water generally has a smaller effective area because the fish has less reaction time to see and pursue a food item.

Feeding lay   The location and position a fish takes as it scans for possible food items.   Fish passively wait and use these sites to ambush unsuspecting prey as they approach.

Holding area   A place where a fish might rest or wait for its next meal to come its way.

Line control   The critical part of removing excess slack in the fly line so as to be able to quickly set the hook should a fish take your fly.

Lining the fish   Casting your fly line over the top of a fish. The heavier fly line hitting the water might easily frighten a fish or at least alert it to your presence.

Mend   A technique, as in an upstream mend, to reduce fly line drag. As the fly hits or is about to hit the water, the angler flips a simple arc in the fly line in an upstream direction. The stream's current will immediately begin to invert the upstream arc. Meanwhile, the fly continues its downstream drift naturally at the same rate as the current.

Nymphal shuck   The shell of an aquatic insect left behind as it changes into an avian lifeform.

Seam   A transitional zone between waters flowing at different rates or directions.

Search pattern   The kind of fly, generally large, colorful or otherwise distinctive, you might use when you have no real idea of where the fish might be or what they may be eating.

Shooting line   Using the weight of the first 30 feet of fly line during the forward part of the cast to help hurl additional lengths of fly line toward more distant targets.

Strip   The action of retrieving the fly line back toward the angler causing the fly to move. Distance of the retrieve can vary from a few inches to several feet and speed can be very slow to very quick depending on how you want the fly to behave.

Stripping guide   The first guide on the fly rod just above the handle.

Strip set   The action of setting the hook by stripping or pulling back on the fly line.   Used with all wet flies.

Tip set   The action of setting the hook by raising the rod tip. Used with floating flies.

Tip top   The last line guide at the very end of the fly rod.

Traditional backcast   The combined action of a rearward and forward cast. This casting technique is most often portrayed by fly anglers on TV or in the movies.

Water haul   The extra energy imparted to the rod caused by the added friction of lifting the fly line from the water.

Wind knot   An overhand or figure 8 knot that develops in the tapered leader and is caused by a tailing loop during the forward casting motion.

24 Greatest Flies

FLY	SIZE	COLOR	UMPQUA ITEM #
1. Adams	12		11302
2. Ant	14	Black or Cinnamon	16811 or 1681
3. Bead Head Hare's Mask Nymph	12		17949
4. Black Gnat Parachute	12		12041 but in black
5. Blue Wing Olive	20		12933
6. Bob's Banger	4/0	Chartreuse or Orange	15383 or 15384
7. CDC Emerger	18	Tan	12121
8. Clouser Minnow	2/0	Chartreuse/White	15385
9. Copper John	14	Copper	14096
10. Crazy Charlie	4	Pink	1530
11. Deceiver	4/0	White/Blue	15485
12. Elk Hair Caddis	12	Olive	10911
13. Grasshopper	6	Yellow	16930
14. Hornberg	8		16412
15. Humpy	12	Royal	11865
16. Mickey Finn	8		16539
17. Muddler Minnow	6		16561
18. Pheasant Tail Nymph	12	Natural	14544
19. Prince Nymph	12		14557
20. Royal Wulff	12		12227
21. Soft Hackle Fly	14		13355
22. Stimulator	6	Orange	11976
23. The Usual	12		
24. Woolly Bugger	6	Olive/Black	13494

LITERATURE REVIEWED

Ainsworth, F. *The Mysteries of Trout Fishing.* Hantsport, N.S.: Lancelot Press, 1987.

Borger, G. *Naturals.* Harrisburg, PA: Stackpole Books, 1980.

Borger, G. *Designing Trout Flies.* Wausau, WI: Tomorrow River Press, 1991.

Clouser, B. *Fly Fishing for Smallmouth.* Mechanicsburg, PA: Stackpole Books, 2007.

Derksen, D.V. (ed.). *Fly Patterns of Alaska.* Portland, OR: Frank Amato Publications, 1993.

Fenner, J.H. *Angling optics: the fish, fisher and fly.* Trout Magazine: 1990 (Spring) p85-95.

Fullum, J. "Fishy". *Fishy's Flies.* Mechanicsburg, PA: Stackpole Books, 2002.

Halverson, M.A. *Stocking trends: a quantitative review of governmental fish stocking in the United States,* 1931-2004. Fisheries 33(2):69-75, 2008.

Harder, J.R. *The Orvis Fly Pattern Index.* New York: Penguin Books, 1990.

Kaufmann, R.K. *Fly Patterns of Umpqua Feather Merchants.* Glide, OR: Umpqua Feather Merchants, 1995.

Leonard, J.E. *Flies.* New York: Nick Lyons Books, 1988.

McCafferty, W.P. *Aquatic Entomology.* Sudbury, MA: Jones and Bartlett Publishers, 1998.

Meck, C.R. and G.A. Hoover.   *Great Rivers — Great Hatches.* Mechanicsburg, PA: Stackpole Books, 1992.

Nemes, S. *Two Centuries of Soft Hackled Flies.* Mechanicsburg, PA: Stackpole Books, 2004.

Soucie, G. *Woolly Wisdom.* Portland, OR: Frank Amato Publications, 2005.

Sousa, R. J. *Learn to Fly Fish in 24 Hours.* Camden, ME: Ragged Mountain Press, 2007.

Talleur, R.W. *Mastering the Art of Fly-Tying.* Harrisburg, PA: Stackpole Books, 1979.

U.S. Department of the Interior, Fish and Wildlife Service. *2006 National Survey of Fishing, Hunting and Wildlife-Associated Recreation.* Washington, DC.

INDEX

FISHING NOTES